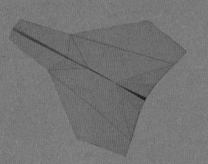

SATE-T-DART—PAGE 79

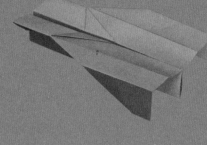

HOUSE FLY—PAGE 72

STACKED OVER LOGAN—PAGE 24

LOCK NOSE DART: SQUARE—PAGE 63

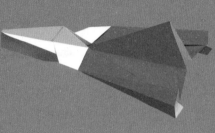

NIFTY FIFTY—PAGE 69

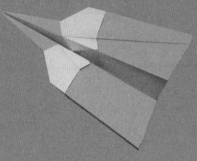

SKY CRUISER—PAGE 54

LOCK NOSE DART: A4—PAGE 63

MAPLE SEED—PAGE 87

SHUTTLE DART—PAGE 32

LOCK NOSE DART: US LETTER B—PAGE 62

RODNEY—PAGE 38

CHUCK FINN—PAGE 26

FUSELAGE-LOCK SWEET DART—PAGE 77

DOUBLE-FLAP NOSE LOCK GLIDER—PAGE 64

PELICAN—PAGE 67

28 INNOVATIVE *ORIGAMI* AIRPLANE DESIGNS
PLANES FOR BRAINS

MICHAEL G. LAFOSSE AND RICHARD L. ALEXANDER, ORIGAMIDO, INC.

TUTTLE Publishing

Tokyo │Rutland, Vermont│ Singapore

This book is lovingly dedicated to the memory of my father, "Jerry" Gerard E. LaFosse.

Published by Tuttle Publishing, an imprint of Periplus Editions (HK) Ltd.

www.tuttlepublishing.com

Library of Congress Cataloging-in-Publication Data

LaFosse, Michael G.
 Planes for brains : 28 innovative origami airplane designs / Michael G. LaFosse, Richard L. Alexander.
   p. cm.
 ISBN 978-4-8053-1149-3 (hardback)
 1. Origami. 2. Airplanes in art. 3. Airplanes--Models. I. Alexander, Richard L., 1953- II. Title.
 TT870.L234383 2011
 736'.982--dc23

                    2011013637

ISBN: 978-4-8053-1149-3

North America, Latin America & Europe
Tuttle Publishing
364 Innovation Drive
North Clarendon, VT 05759-9436 U.S.A.
Tel: 1 (802) 773-8930; Fax: 1 (802) 773-6993
info@tuttlepublishing.com
www.tuttlepublishing.com

Japan
Tuttle Publishing
Yaekari Building, 3rd Floor
5-4-12 Osaki, Shinagawa-ku
Tokyo 141 0032
Tel: (81) 3 5437-0171; Fax: (81) 3 5437-0755
sales@tuttle.co.jp
www.tuttle.co.jp

Asia Pacific
Berkeley Books Pte. Ltd.
61 Tai Seng Avenue
#02-12, Singapore 534167
Tel: (65) 6280-1330; Fax: (65) 6280-6290
inquiries@periplus.com.sg
www.periplus.com

First edition
15 14 13 12 11   5 4 3 2 1   0711EP

Printed in Hong Kong

CONTENTS

A PASSION FOR ORIGAMI AIRPLANES

By Richard Alexander

Above: Unusual colors and papers make origami airships transcend the world of toys.

Right: LEDs light up the Origamido Paper Airplane Boutique!

An eight-year old standing beside me peered into the glass showcase of LaFosse's original paper airplane designs on display at the Peabody Essex Museum. The F-14 Tomcat in the case was being studied intently. An older friend walked up and authoritatively informed us that there was a paper fighter jet on the Internet that was even more awesome. I pointed to the legendary design in the case and said, "Michael LaFosse designed and folded that when your mother was in diapers!" They laughed, and I offered to show them how to fold one of the other LaFosse models in the case. We took a seat one of the tables, and within a couple of minutes, they were flight-testing their Shuttle Darts (see page 32) to great delight.

When I first met Michael LaFosse in 1988, I noticed several boxes stacked in a corner of his living room, and I asked, "What's this?" Michael reached in and proudly presented me with his 1984 Aero-gami pamphlet, *The F-14 TOMCAT: An Origami Model.* Then he picked up a deep-blue, folded fighter jet from the table. This sleek F-14 was particularly amazing for its likeness to the nimble jet, with its twin stabilizers and perfectly proportioned and set wings. He gave it a snap and it shot across the room—fast, straight, and true. I had never seen such an elegant paper airplane design, and I was impressed that he designed and folded it from a single square without making any cuts or using any tape.

Some of us escape into books, music, or even crossword puzzles for relaxation. One of Michael's favorite ways to relax is to immerse himself into what he calls "a blissful world of grappling with the triple-faceted challenge of designing a plane that looks elegant, is interesting to fold, and flies great." After doing this for decades he has developed hundreds of designs spanning a wide variety of styles. His contributions to the present crop of popular paper airplane designs include innovative nose and fuselage locking features, as well as several other clever folding techniques that he has shared at workshops, conventions and contests for years. His inspiring, passionate teaching style has made an impact upon thousands of other paper airplane enthusiasts and designers around the world, most recently at the Red Bull Hangar-7 "Masters of Origami" exhibition and paper airplane workshop in Salzburg, Austria.

I was an early fan of Michael's. As an environmental consultant, I had documented industrial projects with video since 1980, and one look at his F-14 Tomcat booklet made me think that video—rather than just folding diagrams—might be a better way to show how to fold it. Michael's origami F-14 Tomcat was the first model we videotaped him folding. I mounted the camera over the workspace. In this way, Michael and the viewer would see the project in the same orientation on their tables. This also ensured that Michael's verbal references to right, left,

Michael LaFosse poses with his creations under the nose of a particularly fetching North American B-25J "Mitchell" at the Red Bull Hangar-7 "Masters of Origami" exhibition.

top or bottom would make perfect sense. In 1992 we self-published a video collection of his favorite designs, that we called "Planes for Brains." It was a hit.

Then, in 1996, we were asked to develop a first-of-its-kind, beginner's origami video kit for QVC—a popular cable TV shopping channel—and thousands of customers enjoyed folding one of Michael's airplane designs from that set. The same year, we opened our Origamido Studio in the Boston area, and we taught an original LaFosse paper airplane to nearly every group of students that visited. Scouts, homeschoolers, and engineers from Boston's high-tech firms kept coming back for more. Michael seemed to never run out of his own clever paper airplane designs to share with our customers. We held mini-contests by taking turns aligning our toes to the threshold at the hallway door, and sailing the freshly folded planes through the narrow corridor toward the lobby.

Through the years, Origamido Studio developed a whole series of video origami lessons (on DVD, cable TV, and on the Internet), and Tuttle Publishing has embraced origami video instruction by including our DVDs in our latest origami books and kits, including *Money Origami, Trash Origami,* and *Story-gami.* These have proved to be so effective and well-received that we now have several more books and kits with DVDs in development.

We also have a long history of holding paper airplane contests at local libraries and museums, such as the Peabody Essex Museum (PEM) in Salem, Massachusetts. Our first contests began in the early 1990's, and grew to attract hundreds of people for what became an annual family event. Some of the most recent winners (within the oldest age bracket—the "Adult" category) recalled having been winners in the early years of the event, when they were among the youngest contestants (in the "Age 7 and Younger" category).

We hope that your journey might also culminate in a day of fun at a paper airplane contest that you and your friends organize for a special cause or community need. When that smitten youngster comes up to admire (or even critique) a particular paper airplane design on display, we hope that this book and DVD will help you join in the conversation and share your favorite folds with them!

Enjoy!
Richard Alexander, President
ORIGAMIDO, INC.

PAPER AIRPLANE FUN

By Richard Alexander

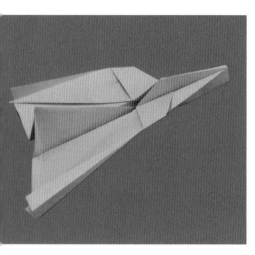

Above: Finding an elegant origami design is a pleasure. Unlimited possibilities make for great fun!

Right: The most successful designs are fun to fold, a pleasure to look at, and a joy to fly.

We love to say that origami (paper folding) comes in many flavors, and every folder seems to have their favorite: greeting cards, animals, boxes, ornaments, jewelry, peace cranes, or dollar bill folds. There is one origami activity that rivals all of these in popularity: the folded paper airplane, perhaps the most satisfying origami flavor of all.

There are many reasons for this: Folding airplanes is fun for any age whether you explore folding alone, with a friend, in teams, or as a family. There is little cost and lots of action. For youngsters, it helps develop many skills and manual dexterity. There may be no better way for them to learn firsthand about cause and effect. Any number of ideas can be quickly conceived, folded, and flight-tested. Learning to apply the discipline of the scientific process can help a folder become more efficient with exploring new designs. Learning new designs challenges your memory. Folding and flying paper airplanes is a pastime you can enjoy for your entire lifetime. Best of all, it is one of the few origami activities that involve getting exercise and enjoying the great outdoors.

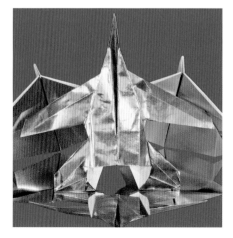

There are two major classes of paper airplanes: the largest group may involve some folding, but also includes assembly from cut-out or punched-out pieces of paper or card, often with slots and tabs, and many require attachments such as tape, glue, or other fasteners. This book is about having fun with the other major class: true origami airplanes folded from a single piece of paper with no cutting, tape, or appliances.

It's a magical experience to transform a handy scrap of paper into a fully functional, soaring sculpture. Whether admired for their bold or graceful lines, superior performance, or amazing acrobatics, a few designs exude a personality of their own. Paper airplane enthusiasts love to share their favorite folding methods, critique each design's looks, and prove the performance of their latest and greatest designs in friendly—but often intense—head-to-head contests.

Perhaps the most famous competition was the "First International Paper Airplane Competition" announced by the *Scientific American* magazine, in 1966. A young Michael LaFosse in Fitchburg, Massachusetts poured over his copy of the Simon and Schuster publication about the event, and, while initially excited by the brains and brouhaha surrounding the contest, he was largely surprised and disappointed by the relatively primitive level of folding technology. Given the state of the art in other origami publications by Randlett, Harbin and Honda, did these origami experts not know about the competition? Perhaps, he thought, there must have been many elegant purely origami entries that just did not fly well enough to qualify. He realized that his own paper airplane repertoire was rather mundane, and began to invest more time developing better origami airplane designs.

Since the early 1970s, Michael LaFosse has been hooked on designing pure origami models, and one of his goals soon became clear: To design interesting, elegant planes that flew well and had reliable landmarks for foolproof folding. The best of these have become his favorite designs, all of which are included in this book.

LaFosse published his first "Aero-gami F-14 Tomcat" design as a pamphlet in 1984, and he placed an ad in the back of the *Popular Science* magazine to sell copies. He also coined the term "Aero-gami" in 1984 for this origami F-14 venture, and he defined it to mean single-sheet, folding only. The origami F-14 Tomcat design quickly became a favorite on Air Force and Naval bases, as well as on engineering college campuses. It looked great, was fun to fold, and flew straight and fast. This design raised eyebrows, and even fighter pilots were impressed with the model and Michael's unusual folding techniques. Similarly, his Art-Deco Wing was so unusual for its time that authors of other origami paper airplane books obtained his permission to publish his innovative designs in their publications—*Wings & Things: Origami that Flies*, by Stephen Weiss (1984, St. Martin's Press); newsletters such as *Fly Paper*, by Charles Peck (1988) and in high tech magazines.

I was swept up in the ultralight aircraft mania of the early 1980's, and fell in love with a one-person, fully retractable, amphibious, fiberglass composite kit called the Diehl Aero-Nautical XTC Cross Terrain Craft. I became a dealer, bought and sold some kits, and built one as an experimental aircraft. This gave me hundreds of hours with pilots, in and around cool warbirds and experimental airplanes at shows, fly-ins, and at several Experimental Aircraft Association (EAA) chapter meetings.

I find folding from diagrams to be frustrating, and I am not alone. Even some college-educated engineers struggle with drawings of complex origami aircraft. Many paper airplane enthusiasts are quite young, and not yet skilled at using technical diagrams, so for them, most origami models are much easier to fold from video instructions. In 1992, we recorded Michael folding his F-14 Tomcat and gave the clip to a neighbor. By using the pause and replay buttons on his video deck, the eight-year-old successfully folded and flew his F-14. This encouraged us to record more of Michael's designs, which allowed us to self-publish a video, "*Planes for Brains.*" A few years later, we followed up with more of his airplanes folded from rectangular office bond (8½ by 11-inch US letter paper) on our video called "*Aerogami.*" We made many of these video lessons available to the public through a pay-per-view website, and then took them to cable TV on Comcast's On Demand "*Activity TV*" series, as well as on the Internet (www.activityTV.com).

Michael has been sharing his designs with many people over the years, and we enjoy meeting them at paper airplane contests and origami conventions. In August, 1999, Michael and I had the opportunity to drive across the USA—from Boston to Seattle—to attend the Origami Regional Conference of America, or "ORCA." One of the younger attendees, named Simon Berry, saw that I was recording video footage of folders explaining their creations, and he volunteered to show me a special, "hybrid" paper airplane he had created. It looked somewhat familiar, and so I asked him how he designed it. Come to find out, a good friend of ours had loaned him Michael LaFosse's first paper airplane video, and Simon had combined elements of Michael's Chuck Finn (see page 26), and the Art-Deco Wing (see page 30). I asked, "What do you call it?" "Simon's Plane!" was his proud reply!

If you love paper airplanes, fold your way through this book, try some of your own modifications, or inject some of Michael's ideas into your original designs. Buy some copies for your friends, and then invite them over for a paper airplane contest cookout in your backyard to see what they've discovered. These friendly competitions increase design expectations and raise the bar for performance. Be prepared for more awesome designs at each subsequent meeting. Friendly competition might even spread to your friends' friends, and can even inspire an entire community.

Now, strap yourself in, because *here we go!*

A sleek Nifty Fifty awaits its maiden voyage.

CHAPTER 1
SELECTING AND
PREPARING YOUR PAPER

First, a word about the basic origami folding essentials: having fun folding paper airplanes doesn't require much. All you need is:

- A few sheets of suitable paper.
- A clean, hard, folding surface.
- Good lighting.
- Something to trim your paper to size.
- Something to help you make sharp, accurate creases.

The last two items are not essential. We can easily trim paper without tools by creasing and tearing, but the last item is worth a little discussion. Great planes have properly-placed, sharp creases. Generally, the back of your thumbnail works fine for installing creases, but some folders prefer to use their favorite "folding tool," a handy device that comes in a variety of shapes and lengths, available in craft stores. They may be plastic, or fashioned of wood, stone or bone (bone folders), but there are plenty of no-cost substitutes: Young children with tiny fingers, and teens sporting fashionable fingernail artistry, can still make sharp creases using the bottom of a spoon. Beginners can define a crease line by folding the paper up against a straight edge, but soon you will easily use several fingers to roll the paper between two points before you press down on the curl to commit to the crease placement.

Paper airplanes demand precise placement of the creases, so don't skip the introductory Symbols Key and folding tips presented in the next chapter, even if you have other paper folding experience. If the models you fold do not fly well, go back and master the simple, but critical folding techniques. In a short amount of time you will learn a lot about paper, develop fundamental folding skills, understand the symbols in an origami diagram, and learn what makes these paper airplane designs so neat.

paper selection

Paper selection for competition may be important, but for practice paper, just look in your recycle bin. You can find suitable paper for airplanes nearly everywhere. The designs presented in this book work well with the most widely available paper types: letter-size, 20-pound bond, and common sizes of square "origami paper." Printer and copy paper is fine for any project in this book. If more types are available, use the heavier papers for simpler designs, and save the larger, lighter-weight papers for the more complex designs.

Paper is often supplied at a paper airplane competition (which simplifies the judging) but sometimes you will be given a choice. For competition, first select the best airplane design for the category (e.g., greatest distance, greatest time aloft, best aerobatic, best target accuracy, coolest design, etc.) and then select the paper for that design that works best for you. When you have a choice of papers, consider:

- Paper format
- Squareness
- Weight
- Thickness
- Foldability
- Rigidity
- Aesthetics (color, finish, graphics)

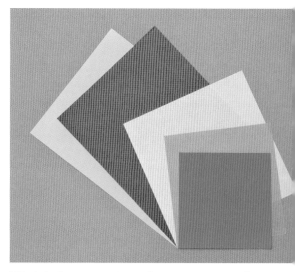

This photo shows an assortment of common paper rectangle types: square, 8 ½ by 11-inch US office paper and A4 letter paper.

paper formats

Most published origami paper airplanes have been designed to be folded from one of these three common, handy rectangles: square origami paper; 8 ½ by 11-inch office paper used in North America; or A4 letter paper used most everywhere else.

We have included designs for all three formats. We have also included instructions on how to produce these three rectangles from stock so that you may enjoy folding all of the designs, no matter what format of paper is handy. For practical purposes, rectangular papers can be expressed in terms of absolute measurements, aspect ratio and diagonal angle measurements. Understanding these expressions will allow you to scale rectangles into larger or smaller sizes as needed.

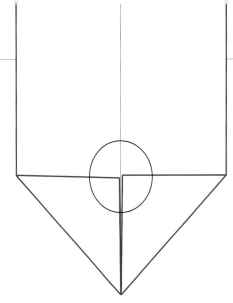

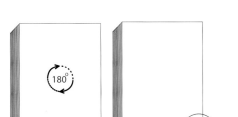

Avoid performance-affecting inconsistencies, such as the one shown in this illustration, by taking care to use only accurately, cut rectangles.

Rotate part of a stack of paper 180 degrees, square one end, and then check the other end for squareness.

You can also inspect squareness by folding a piece of paper in half to make sure that the loose corners line up on both sides.

squareness

Many folders blame themselves if their folding seems off, without ever considering that the paper may not be cut properly. When you open a package of square origami paper, remove a few sheets from the center of the stack, rotate it 90 degrees, and align the ream with one edge of the stack on the table. If the sheets you turned stick out, either on top, or on a side, you know that paper was not square. Similarly, when you open a ream of office paper, turn a few sheets from the center around 180 degrees and align one end with a tap on the table. Look at the top edge to see if the rotated sheets are even along the top, or if they stick out at either side.

You can also try the following folding experiment. Take a sheet of letter paper and fold it in half, long edge to long edge. Are the edges and corners of the top layer matching those of the layer beneath?

Next, unfold the paper and form a simple "airplane point" at one end of the sheet by folding the two halves of a short edge to meet at the center crease. Do the two square corners meet?

Unfold the paper and try the same thing at the other end. It is not uncommon for a sheet to fail these tests for trueness. In most cases, trim discrepancies are slight and can be accommodated for folded paper airplanes. However, when the trim error is off by several millimeters you should consider re-trimming the paper to true it up. This will be especially important for performance-critical contest entries.

To learn if your store-bought origami paper is acceptably symmetrical simply fold the sheet in half diagonally, corner to corner. The edges and the free corner of the top layer should match those of the bottom layer.

Thickness

The planes in this book were designed to be folded from many common types and sizes of paper—either origami paper or 20-pound letter bond—but a general guide will be to use thinner papers on the complex models and thicker on the simplest ones.

There is also the issue of *relative thickness*, which can be expressed as a ratio of thickness to area. You can use a thicker paper if the area is increased, but thinner stock must be used if you decrease the area of the sheet.

If you were to graph the variables of the acceptable planes, you would determine the designs' acceptable range of relative thickness. Each paper airplane design will have an optimum size for a given thickness. When designing new paper planes it is wise to keep the technical handling of the folds well within the doable limits of the paper with which you are experimenting. Some paper folding design plans may accumulate many layers in certain places, such as the nose or the leading edge of the wings. Choose paper thin enough to accommodate the folding in the thickest places of the model. If an airplane folded from thick paper does not perform well, perhaps that design should be folded from a larger sheet, in order to bring the design back into the "doable range" (or *window of acceptability*).

weight

Most office and printing stocks fall into one of two types: "*Bond*," and "*Offset.*" Each type has different weights, sold in packs, or reams, of 500 sheets. The ream is marked with a number indicating the weight, such as 20-pound (abbreviated 20 #, 20 lb, etc.). When you lift a 500-sheet ream of 20-pound bond, the first thing you notice is that it cannot possibly weigh 20 pounds. That is because all grades of bond are labeled with the weight, in pounds, of a much larger ream measuring 11 by 22 inches—which is called the basis size for bond papers.

It's confusing, but reams of so-called "offset" paper stocks (including "book," "text" and "coated" stock) used in professional printing presses are made by different machinery, so their weight is described by a different basic size sheet: 25 by 38 inches. You can't compare the two types by only considering the area. The 50-pound offset stock is slightly lighter than 20-pound bond because the machinery that makes the offset paper uses a process that makes it thinner and denser.

The system is useful when comparing the weights of the same types of paper: 24-pound bond is 20% heavier than 20-pound bond (24-20=4; 4/20= 20%), and 60-pound offset is 20% heavier than 50-pound offset paper (60-50=10; 10/50=20%).

Metric units are more direct. When paper "weight" is described in grams per square meter, this removes confusion, but we are probably stuck with knowing and using at least a few different systems for a while.

PLANES FOR BRAINS

Special planes intended for photography or display often benefit from the use of crisp tracing paper, which really shows off the intricate folds and precise workmanship.

Only simple, large models can be folded from heavy papers. When you fold the same design from different weights of papers with the same area, those from heavier papers will glide farther, but are less likely to look neat because of bunching caused by the increased thickness. When you lift an airplane and launch it, your arm is imparting a force on the mass of the plane. Those folded from heavier papers have greater mass, but essentially the same area and resistance to air molecules. Other variables being equal, increased mass translates to increased potential energy, and greater distance.

Foldability

How well does the paper take a crease? How many times can the paper be folded back and forth before it splits or cracks? How long does that crease stay crisp? Many papers today are coated with plastic, paint, clay, varnish, wax or even silicone. Some are fused to metal or plastic films. Heavily coated papers and foils are unforgiving of poor technique, so it is important to choose papers that fit your folding skills. At the very least, it is fun and instructive to test an origami airplane on many kinds of papers. This is when the paper is your best teacher.

Rigidity

Rigid paper planes are generally more efficient and fly better than floppy planes. The rigidity can come from the weight and size of the paper, but also the folding method. Compare a paper towel to a sheet of letter paper. Each was formulated and manufactured differently to best suit a particular need. A soft paper towel does not make a good paper airplane: it would be too floppy. However, a paper plane that is folded from a very large sheet of office paper, say four times its typical size, could be so heavy, that the shape of the flaps and wings would distort.

Moisture in the air changes from day to day and also affects paper's rigidity. On very humid days, you may have noticed that fins flutter and wings droop—this change of shape

affects motion. As a deformation propagates along the surface, it results in extra wind resistance and unwanted drag. Energy expended to flex the structure is energy drained from the momentum (forward path of force), shortening or even stalling a flight. Unequal distortions to wing or fin can also result in an erratic path. Using slightly smaller sheets of paper can improve rigidity, as can choosing models that have multi-layered wings with several folded edges.

Rigid wings of balsa or from composites of paper card will always perform better than pure origami planes. Nevertheless, origami airplanes can produce some impressive and very satisfying performances.

Aesthetics Impact Performance

Color pigments, printing inks, and toners on the paper may have a small, but measurable impact on a paper airplane's mass (and therefore density), surface roughness and symmetry. Besides these technical aspects, the aesthetics of a paper airplane's appearance may influence the crowd and psych-out the competition. Do drivers of bright red cars receive more speeding tickets? Does the car's color somehow motivate the driver to hit the gas pedal harder? Do people who are more likely to speed select car colors of the more aggressive hues? Use plain white paper if you subscribe to the maxims "Beauty is only skin-deep," or "Don't judge a book by its cover." This lets you appreciate the elegance of the plane's lines and geometry. Aesthetics can also be a function of age and culture, so you must decide how to play this card.

Putting It All Together

Paper selection depends upon why you are folding the model. If you are just practicing, use anything available. If you have plenty of used copier paper handy in a recycle bin, begin by learning the models that work well from that format. If you are supplying the paper for an airplane competition, a ream of 20-pound office paper is readily available and inexpensive, so that is what most people use. If a local printing company will donate the paper, ask for 50-pound offset, but don't be fussy. Thank them profusely, even if they give you misprints. (There are plenty of sponsorship opportunities here.)

When folding paper airplane models for display or photography, we sometimes prefer to fold thin, crisp, white tracing paper with a hard surface finish (this stock is translucent, which shows off the interesting lines of internal folds). These models may not fly as well because the paper is light. Although the creases look sharp, they are also weak. One final note: terms such as "bond," "offset" or "letter" paper are generic. You should expect quality to vary between different brands, and even paper formulations of the same brand can be changed from time to time. Test, test, test!

Testing Papers

Trial and error is a good teacher, but using the scientific method will help you to organize your investigations and better evaluate your findings. The following is a simple experiment to test papers against airplane designs.

1. Choose one design.
2. Fold several versions with the same size, but different types of paper.
3. Fly each and make notes about their performance.
4. If performance correlates with a given characteristic (say, weight), fold more models with even heavier paper, to determine where the performance benefits trail off.
5. Note the weight that gives you the best performance.
6. You can run the tests again with the same design but with a different variable, say square area.

Eventually you will be able to match paper type, size and airplane design to get your best performance. Remember, you are a variable, too!

Now that you know more about paper types and choices, you will be rewarded by being able to make better choices and evaluations, whether at a paper airplane competition or for your own enjoyment.

Fold the same design at different sizes to discover which scale works best for a given plane.

Additional Paper Handling Tips

Here are some additional tips to optimize your folding experience:

- Make sure your hands are clean and dry. Sorry for nagging, but paper can easily absorb oils and moisture from your skin.
- Leave the paper in the packaging. Paper left out of its packaging is subject to damage from a variety of agents.
- Examine both sides of the paper carefully. Some papers have a finished side that is smoother than the other side. Know which side will show when you fold your model. We have color-coded our diagrams to help you: White is the inside of the model and the colored side is the predominant display side of the finished model.
- When using pages from discarded magazine or calendars, or other "trash" papers, make sure the sheet is completely flat and that the corners are square. Trim to remove any ugly wrinkles or bruised edges.
- If you are adding graphics to your paper, be sure to leave enough time for toner to cool, or inks to dry before folding.

Incidentally, papers that pass through the heated rollers of toner-based printers and copy machines seem to become crisper and make better planes.

- Planes that sit around for a while will tend to lose the sharpness in their creases, making them sloppy, unbalanced and not airworthy. Always refresh your creases and check symmetry before flight.

Preparing Your Paper

In the following sections we provide several methods for trimming paper to the proportions used in this book. Use a straightedge or ruler, pencil, and scissors or paper cutter, to easily scale your papers, making larger or smaller sheets of each format. You can use any of the numbers, displayed with each of the rectangular icons in this section, as factors to scale or trim your paper.

Square Paper

Square paper is the simplest format to prepare, and you can even do it without any tools. This is perhaps why the square is the most common format for origami design. Vertical and horizontal sides are equal, so the ratio of a square's adjacent sides is 1:1. To prepare the largest possible square from any rectangle simply fold one of the short edges to match an adjacent long edge. If you do not want to make a diagonal crease, use two sheets of the same size rectangle, overlapping them at one corner while aligning the second perpendicular to other. Trim the excess of each for two clean squares.

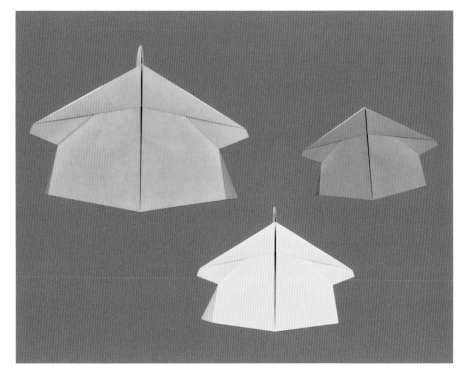

The technical specifications of a square.

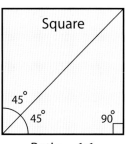

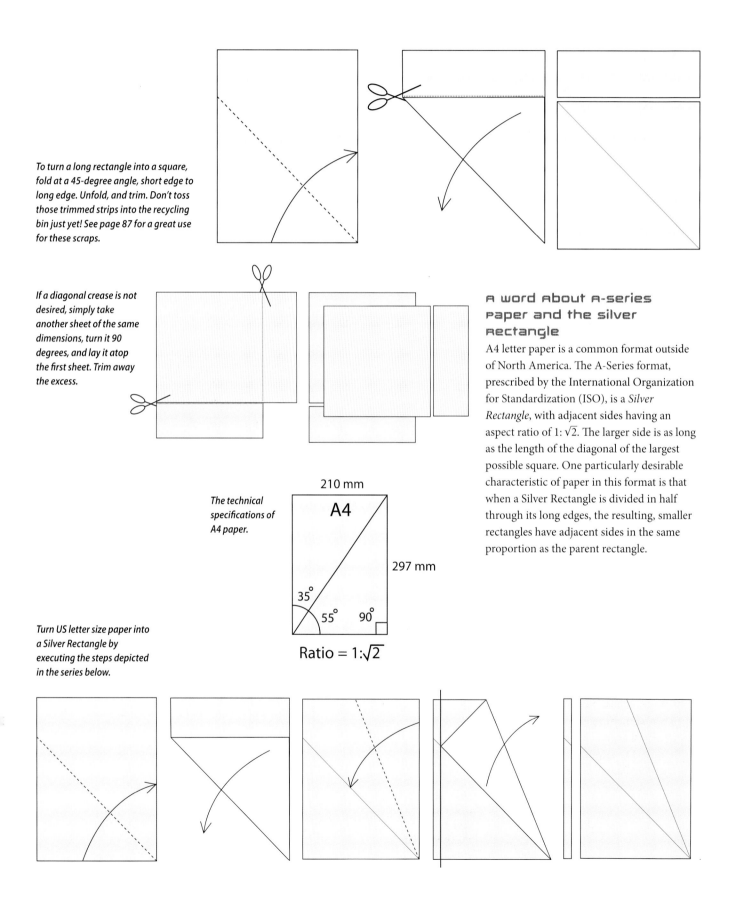

To turn a long rectangle into a square, fold at a 45-degree angle, short edge to long edge. Unfold, and trim. Don't toss those trimmed strips into the recycling bin just yet! See page 87 for a great use for these scraps.

If a diagonal crease is not desired, simply take another sheet of the same dimensions, turn it 90 degrees, and lay it atop the first sheet. Trim away the excess.

A word about A-series paper and the silver rectangle

A4 letter paper is a common format outside of North America. The A-Series format, prescribed by the International Organization for Standardization (ISO), is a *Silver Rectangle*, with adjacent sides having an aspect ratio of 1: $\sqrt{2}$. The larger side is as long as the length of the diagonal of the largest possible square. One particularly desirable characteristic of paper in this format is that when a Silver Rectangle is divided in half through its long edges, the resulting, smaller rectangles have adjacent sides in the same proportion as the parent rectangle.

The technical specifications of A4 paper.

210 mm

A4

297 mm

35°

55°

90°

Ratio = 1:$\sqrt{2}$

Turn US letter size paper into a Silver Rectangle by executing the steps depicted in the series below.

scale any rectangle

It is useful to know how to cut smaller or larger rectangles of the same proportion to make paper planes that perform well and look better on display. No matter the kind of rectangle, the method is the same. Inscribe a diagonal line that spans two corners of the rectangle. Intersect this line at any desired point, and connect that point back to each edge with perpendicular cut lines leading to the vertical and horizontal edges.

forming a us letter proportion from a square

Letter paper commonly found in North America measures 8 ½ inches by 11 inches. You can measure and cut these rectangles from odd stock and you can use the above method (see "Scale Any Rectangle") to make larger or smaller examples. However, there is a quick approximation you can use to make rectangles with proportions close enough for the projects in this book. Fold the square in half, edge to edge, but make only a pinch to mark the center. Open. Fold one edge to the pinch and trim off the resulting flap. The remaining rectangle will have an aspect ratio of 1: 0.75, which is acceptably close to the proportions of US letter paper (1: 0.77) to be used for the majority of the planes in this book.

forming a us letter proportion from an a4 sheet

A4 paper is handy to paper plane enthusiasts in Europe and Asia. Though some of the models in this book can be easily adapted to the A4 sheet, most of the US letter models will look better and fly best if folded from rectangles with those proportions. It is an easy task to trim the A4 sheet to the correct proportions: simply cut a 1-inch (2 ½-centimeter) strip from a short edge of the sheet. Incidentally, these slightly smaller models fly extremely well!

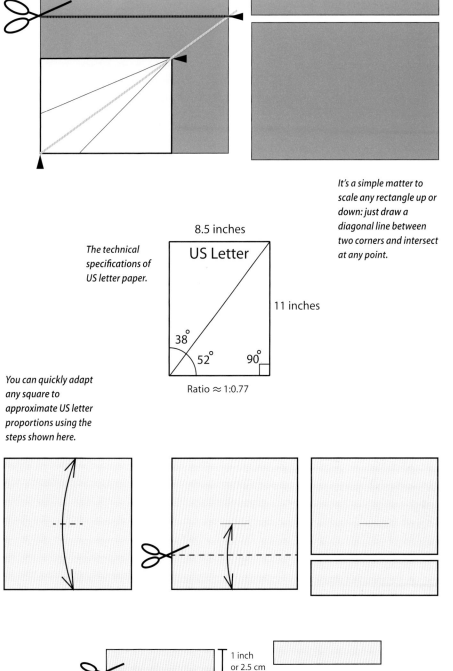

It's a simple matter to scale any rectangle up or down: just draw a diagonal line between two corners and intersect at any point.

The technical specifications of US letter paper.

8.5 inches

US Letter

11 inches

38°   52°   90°

Ratio ≈ 1:0.77

You can quickly adapt any square to approximate US letter proportions using the steps shown here.

1 inch or 2.5 cm

A4

US Letter proportion

You can quickly convert any A4 size sheet to US letter size using the steps shown here.

CHAPTER 2
MASTERFUL FOLDING TECHNIQUES

Crisp, precise and neatly folded paper airplanes look best and fly best. Making sharp creases without bruising the paper also takes a degree of skill, which comes with practice. It is also true that freshly folded planes fly best. Here are some tips that will help you fold neatly.

creasing carefully

Assuming that the corners are square, neat folding begins with properly aligning the parts of the paper before committing the fold with a crease.

Secure the alignment by first pressing at the middle of the fold, and then slide from the center to the right, (if using your right hand), or to the left (if using your left hand). Return to the center and create the other half of the crease. This simple technique decreases the amount of *creep* (or deviation) away from the fold line.

Whether you use a folding tool or just your fingers, first coax the paper gently to decrease the radius of the bend uniformly along the crease line, adjusting the placement several times before committing the decision with a fold, then sharpen the crease.

Once paper planes have had a chance to sit for a while, the folds will begin to relax. Dramatic changes in temperature and humidity make this happen rapidly. Always re-sharpen your creases before flying a plane that has been sitting for a while.

Carefully line up the corners. Press the middle of the fold, and then slide to the corners. Sharpen the creases with the back of a fingernail, a spoon or other folding tool.

mastering the inside-reverse fold

We often use *Inside-reverse Folds* in this book for wing development. This technique can be troublesome for beginners, both in the interpretation of the diagrams and in its execution. The "reverse" happens when a *valley crease* is changed to form a *mountain crease*, and vise-versa. The "inside" part implies that this crease change will involve the movement of some of the layers between others. The video demonstrations should be helpful, but in the interest of reinforcing good technique we have prepared a series of photos that correspond to diagrammed Steps 18–20 in the Flying Fox instructions, seen on page 46.

mastering the squash fold

The *Squash Fold* is another important origami technique. It involves the opening and flattening of a multi-layer flap. Our photos correspond to Steps 5–6 from the Art-Deco Wing instructions, seen on page 31.

THE INSIDE-REVERSE FOLD

1. The fold to be reversed is here, shown as a valley crease.

2. The crease and its attached layers are moved, inside-out along the prescribed limits.

3. The completed Inside-reverse Fold.

THE SQUASH FOLD

1. The flap to be squashed is raised perpendicular.

2. The flap is then opened and flattened down. It is important to keep the squash symmetrical, and to keep the supporting layers from spreading at the base during the maneuver. Use one hand to stabilize the base and the other to flatten the flap.

3. The completed Squash Fold.

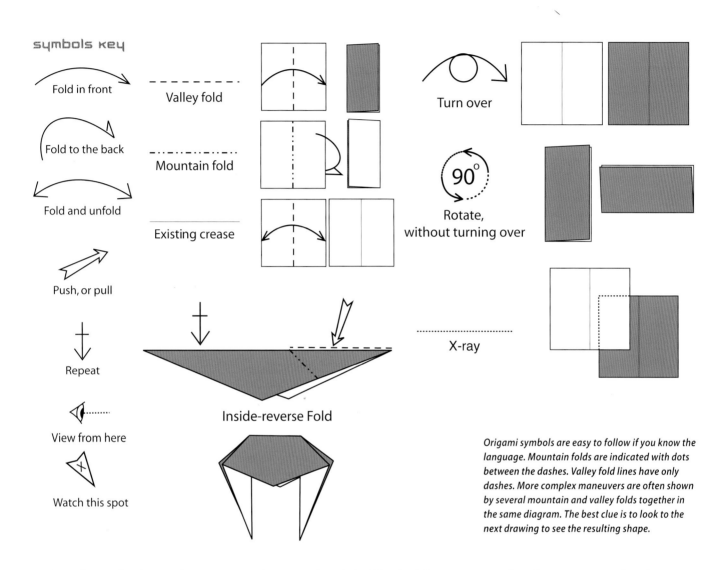

symbols key

Fold in front — Valley fold

Fold to the back — Mountain fold

Fold and unfold — Existing crease

Push, or pull

Repeat

View from here

Watch this spot

Turn over

90° Rotate, without turning over

X-ray

Inside-reverse Fold

Origami symbols are easy to follow if you know the language. Mountain folds are indicated with dots between the dashes. Valley fold lines have only dashes. More complex maneuvers are often shown by several mountain and valley folds together in the same diagram. The best clue is to look to the next drawing to see the resulting shape.

origami symbols & diagrams

Origami instructions are most often explained by line drawings, called "diagrams." The use of specialized arrows and dashed lines—often referred to as the "*Yoshizawa-Randlett System*"—has been universally adopted. This system has made the diagramming of origami models efficient and effective. Since origami is an international pastime, one need not be able to read any explanatory text in order to learn an origami project. Take a few moments to become familiar with the key and refer to it frequently if you are new to origami diagrams. Knowing how to read origami diagrams takes time to develop, but it will unlock thousands of new designs for you. The accompanying DVD will aid you in your understanding of how to interpret origami diagrams, so keep the book handy while you use the video lessons.

when in doubt, look ahead

The best advice we can give to novice readers of origami diagrams it to always read two steps at a time. The valley and mountain crease lines in the first drawing show you where the creases will occur and the arrows will point the direction to move a flap, edge or corner to make these creases come to be. It is in the next drawing that you will always see the result.

don't overlook the details

Some people forget to look carefully at the details, or they think that they understand what they saw and they rush on and make a mistake or leave out a step. When this happens it is best to retrace your steps and see if you have missed something in a previous diagram. If you manage to fold the entire plane all the way through, but it does not fly well, you may have missed a small but important detail. Usually, it is an important flap or some other control surface that has been omitted.

CHAPTER 3
HOW TO DESIGN EXCEPTIONAL PAPER AIRPLANES

By Michael G. LaFosse

Looks are important. If an origami airplane looks interesting, you are more likely to take the trouble fold it. We hope you selected this book because you liked the looks of some of the planes in this collection. I feel a great sense of satisfaction when I design a plane that becomes a popular classic, but gems can be few and far between—even years in the making. I estimate that I have explored several hundred design ideas, yet I have named only about 50, and perhaps just half of those have achieved the "classic" level of popular acclaim. Some of the others looked great, but if they don't fly well, why bother?

My first published design was the F-14 Tomcat fighter. I, like many designers of paper airplanes, was once obsessed with trying to make pure origami models of *real* aircraft. This is not a problem unless you expect them to fly well. My F-14 does fly well, but it took me years to let go of the idea that I had to include a canopy, twin engines, and realistically proportioned twin tail fins just like the real F-14. I wanted the detail, but even more, I wanted it to fly well. Eventually I refined the model into a suitable compromise—something that would be a successful glider on its own, but still allude unmistakably to the F-14 Tomcat as my inspiration.

Let's first examine what we think about how a successful origami paper airplane should look. Paper airplanes with clean, geometric designs are my favorites, whether they look like anything that exists in real life or not (yet).

- In general, the paper airplane should look "right." And by that I mean that no part of its design looks out of place, awkward or superfluous. Some may have a generally pleasing appearance, and some may look menacing, but whatever the character, it must look right, and not unfinished, or overdone. Arriving at this point can be quite difficult.
- The model should be balanced. Of course it must be physically balanced from side to side, but also visually balanced. Does it have a harmonious blend of design elements? Are the lines elegant, and do they relate to other areas, shapes, and angles? Are they without any distracting clutter from unnecessary folds, flaps, or facets?
- The overall composition should be interesting, fresh, and compelling. Simple darts are elegant and fun. They fly great, but people are always more interested in something new or fresh.
- The design should evoke action, and communicate, with honesty, what the sculpture is supposed to do. Will it shoot through the air like a laser beam, or float gracefully on the breeze before it glides to a gentle perch atop a distant neighbor's lawn?

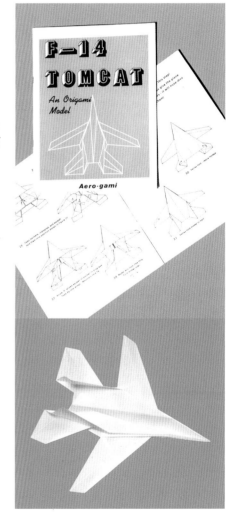

Top: Michael LaFosse's first foray into origami publishing came in 1984 with this popular pamphlet.

Above: Like the full-size Grumman warbird, beautiful lines and amazing performance are the hallmarks of the LaFosse F-14 Tomcat model. Fold this amazing plane for yourself! (Page 51)

PLANES FOR BRAINS

Specific design "rules" for decent paper airplanes are a bit easier to define:

- Folded edges look cleaner and stay in shape better than exposed, cut edges.
- Lines (creases) must exist for a reason. Superfluous creases are distracting and can cause drag or structural weakness.
- Layers should obey the direction of the airflow (and not trap air).
- Large wing areas need to be rationally supported by structure. Folding edges over several times will increase rigidity, adding support.
- A reasonable place to hold the plane for launching should be part of its design.
- The aspects, including the underside, should be tidy. Extraneous flaps can cause drag.
- Control surfaces (flaps, spoilers, etc.) should ideally be well defined and easy to adjust.

Not surprisingly, the folding method necessary to achieve elegant plane designs is usually elegant as well. As we perfect a design, we are pursuing as much sensible geometry and reproducible maneuvers as necessary to produce a pleasing form. Each type of rectangle has its own bag of tricks that help to achieve a harmonious effect.

Sometimes a design looks great, but performance is lacking. We reject those too, because the design is incomplete. Sometimes the model is tweaked for hours before either it succeeds, or we abandon it and move on.

I find it helpful to give the brain a rest when refining a design. Many successful designs result from combining a fresh idea with an earlier design approach. Many years may pass before an earlier design gets a fresh look, but it is usually a great improvement.

There is no doubt that some of my favorite designs were influenced by my early fascination with finned automobiles, rocket ships, and especially the warbirds that my father photographed while he was in the Air Force in the 1950's, but over the years, one thing has emerged: it is not important for my origami airplane designs to resemble anything from the real world of aircraft.

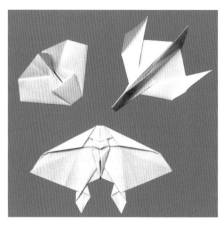

Here are three of my "abandoned" models, of which I am yet very fond. They fly passably well, but they are not trouble free—often requiring lots of improvised adjustments.

Design for Performance

The fact that most paper airplane designs fly best when mass is piled into the nose certainly has influenced the designs in this book. There are only a few easy ways to do this, and each technique also presents certain options for adding cockpits, nose-locks, and foreword wings or canards.

Let's start from the beginning. Take a piece of paper and wad it tightly. Throw it as far as you can. Measure the distance. Can you design a way to fold the paper to travel farther? Paper airplanes certainly give the paper a more interesting trip. When you launch a set of folded paper airplanes all with the same force, the energy from your arm transferred to the paper is drained away by air resistance, and the plane will do one of two things: Either the wing will stall and the plane will drop, or it will gently lower its nose, and develop enough forward momentum to generate lift, pull out of the dive, and land gracefully.

The Drop Test

Many paper airplanes are to be launched with great force, and others seem to need very little forward thrust at all. One of the most interesting ways to explore the aerodynamics of a design is to conduct what we call the "drop test."

Each plane has a balance point along the centerline where it could be supported on the tip of a pin. Locate this balance point by holding the plane with the tips of your two index fingers, pointing to each other, under the wings.

When you look down on a paper airplane from directly above, you will notice more wing area aft (behind) the balance point. If you were to hold a paper airplane from the balance point and release it to gravity with no forward motion by just dropping it, the nose should encounter less air resistance and rotate downward. If the plane hits the ground almost directly below the drop point, its wing shape has little or no lift. The design may be a great dart, and may do well in a distance contest if you have a great arm. If the plane pulls out of the dive and stays upright during a glide, the design is said to be stall-resistant, or self-correcting. Some designs will porpoise, or nose up, then down, then up, etc. Experiment with trimming the designs by tweaking the trailing edges of the wings so that they react predictably.

Designing for Distance vs. Hang Time (Time Aloft)

Why are there so many different designs for real aircraft? A visit to an aviation museum quickly reveals that different planes were built for different purposes. Spy planes are sleek and fast to fly high and avoid detection. Acrobatic planes (these are often biplanes) carry lots of wing with exaggerated control surfaces and powerful engines.

Folded paper planes generally fall into two performance categories based upon aspect configuration. The first includes the long and slender darts, and these are generally the distance performers; they are also good for use in precision or target contests, much like a dart or a spear. Generally, rigid planes with low profile wings will allow you to throw the plane hard, without it immediately distorting or stalling.

The other category includes the wings—short, wide planes. These planes

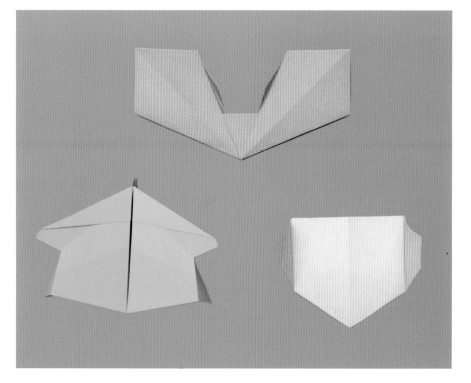

The planes above fit the general proportions of "wider than long" and are typically used for long, slow gliding and stunts.

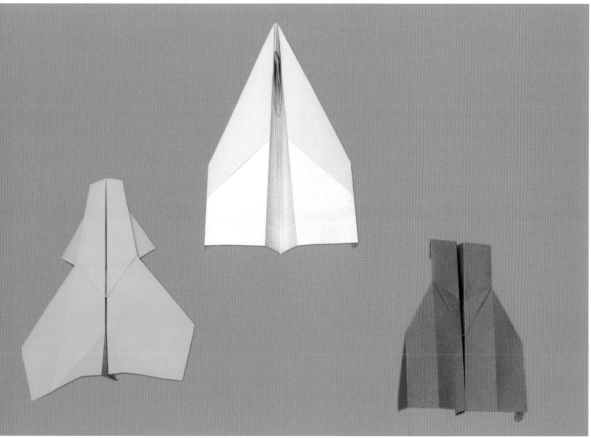

The planes to the left fit the general proportions of "longer than wide" for fast-flying straight, distance and targeted flights.

PLANES FOR BRAINS

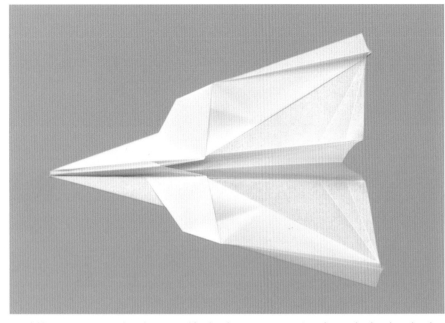

Fun folding sequences—such as the one used for this Sky Cruiser (page 54)— rely upon landmarks rather than measuring tools.

model designed for folding fun will have several satisfying moments. What makes these models so much fun to fold?

Landmarks. A direct, logical sequence of shapes and maneuvers that makes good use of reliable landmarks, such as corners, edges, and crease marks, is easier to remember, and therefore more fun. Every new shape presents itself with a few obvious choices for placing the next crease. Placement should be inherent, rather than relying on measuring with tools. We think this lends a quality of intrinsic perfection to the design.

Set-ups. Sometimes there are favorite maneuvers that require predictable pre-creasing, or set-up steps, as in steps 9–15 in the Flying Fox (page 45). The payoff is usually a twist, sink, pullout, or collapse (a good thing) that is the highlight of the folding experience. These set-ups can be applied to other designs in need of improvement or variation.

The unexpected. Logical and direct is always good, but an unexpected transformation adds interest to the folding process. The nose-lock in the Shuttle Dart and wing forming steps, 14–23, in the F-14 Tomcat are examples.

"Zen." Folding is tactile fun. A good origami design that has an easy flow, cadence, or rhythm is a pleasure to fold. Some feel inner peace by admiring how the geometry changes, and it can be quite

are the acrobats, and are generally capable of long glides. The "wings" in this book include the Stormin' Norman, Art-Deco Wing, Chuck Finn, and the Double Flap Nose Lock Glider—each flying much like a hang-glider. Some planes, though longer than they are wide, still perform best with a gentle launch. These planes also belong in the wing class, despite their appearance. Some can be launched to climb high and then slowly descend.

Designing a Fun Folding Sequence

Most people fold paper airplanes for the joy of flying them, but more than a few also enjoy the process of folding itself. It is like singing a favorite song. Sometimes we fold a plane to share a design with a friend, sometimes we fold because it just feels good, and sometimes we do it to show off. When a student folds one of our designs over and over, we assume that the sequence is fun. A

Strategic pre-creasing allows for this fairly complex 3-D folded structure to be formed with little effort.

The structure is folded to the underside in preparation for the final collapse.

Pre-creases make the shape easy to flatten into the form that will allow the development of the wings and a nose lock.

Top Right: Pre-creases have been installed in preparation for an inside-petal fold.

Middle Right Above: For this step, the easiest way is to open the paper, wide; and to trust that the installed creases will remember their place after performing the inside-petal fold!

Middle Right Below: Well done! This necessary step trims the leading edges of the wings and provides freer movement of the paper layers, allowing them to be positioned further forward on the fuselage.

Bottom Right: A wing in its proper position, ready for final development.

meditative. Others call folding "dancing with the paper," and like a dance it can be both stimulating and relaxing at the same time.

control surface tweaking and optimization

All of the models in this book have been developed to just "fold and fly." They do, however, feature control surfaces designed into the planes that you should know about and appreciate. Control surfaces are adjustable features that let you correct an undesirable flight. The slightest adjustment is all that is necessary, and what you do to one side you will usually need to do to the other, to balance the plane.

Prerequisites: Straight flights begin by ensuring that the plane is actually symmetrical: one wing should not be lower than the other, and all fins and flaps are set to match their counterparts. Wings often have multiple layers, so be sure that the layers of one wing are no more or less open than those of the other. Vertical stabilizers usually need to be perpendicular to the horizontal plane of the wings, and they must be symmetrical.

Elevators and Elevons: An elevator is a flap at the back edge of a horizontal tail wing; an elevon is a flap at the back edge of a delta-type wing. These control the pitch of the flight path, whether the plane will fly up, level, or down. Planes with elevons have no separate horizontal tail wings. Most of the

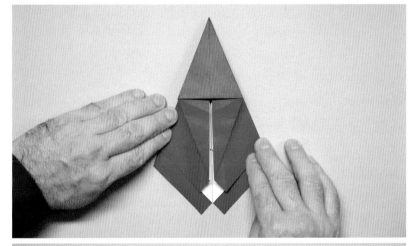

PLANES FOR BRAINS

models in this book are such planes. Adjusting the elevator or elevon up will make the nose of the plane head down; conversely, adjusting these flaps down will make the nose go up. Setting one flap higher than the other may make the plane turn right or left. It could also cause the plane to spiral. Experimenting with elevator and elevon settings is fun and rewarding.

The control surfaces indicated in these illustrations can be manipulated to improve flight characteristics.

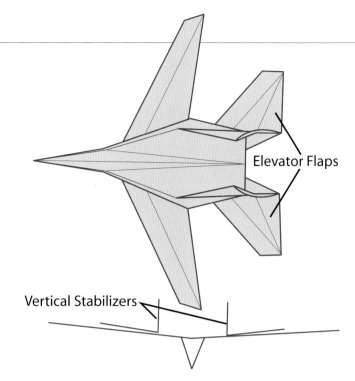

Elevator Flaps

Vertical Stabilizers

HOW TO FLY YOUR PAPER AIRPLANE

To throw any plane that has a keel below the wings: Hold forward of the center, aim like a dart and throw with a smooth release.

Throwing planes that lack a lower keel is not a problem. Hold forward of the center at a convenient point on the leading edge of a wing. The pose is largely horizontal, but at a comfortable angle for your wrist. End with a smooth release.

Be aware of your surroundings. Do not go into areas where you are not welcome or that are dangerous.

Throwing. What could be simpler than throwing a paper airplane? You'd think it is as easy as just giving it a toss. However, if you pass the same plane to a variety of contestants with their toes on the throwing line, and then ask each to launch the plane, you'll see that some people have it, and others don't.

Is it pure strength? Probably not. Throwing most paper airplanes with all your might causes distortion and turbulence in

the air. Like all sports, launching a paper airplane well is a practiced art, a learned skill. Paper airplanes, like all sports equipment, will have various design and performance qualities. Each kind of paper airplane will have an optimum launch style and speed for a good flight.

The release of the plane is just as important as the proper grip and throw. Some planes do best with a constant-speed arm, while others tolerate an accelerating

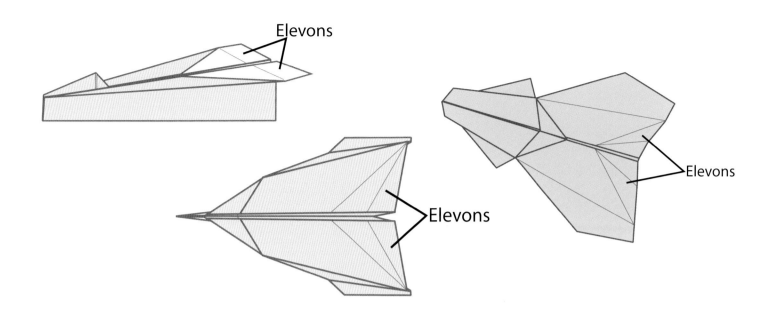

Elevons

Elevons

Elevons

Hold wings at the back edge and launch above your head with a gentle push. Elevated launch points work best.

Wings can also be launched nose first, straight up into the air. This will allow for you to put more energy into your throw, making the wing loop before gliding.

arm. Some respond to a wrist snap at the end. In general, it is important to allow a smooth release and a directed aim. Throwing a paper airplane can be as complex as throwing a baseball, and just think of how many ways there are to do that, even when the ball's mass and size must conform to a highly regulated, uniform standard. Full body movement is also important. Many competitors take two steps before release, adding the forward momentum of the arm's mass besides the motion of the arm muscles.

In the final analysis, throwing a paper airplane for optimum performance is just something one has to practice, like hitting a golf ball or riding a skateboard. And like many other sports, paper airplanes can provide fun exercise. There are no greens fees, and your health insurance card is much less likely to get a workout.

Do not throw your planes at bystanders; a paper plane can be a dangerous and painful missile!

AIRPLANE #1
STACKED OVER LOGAN

By Michael G. LaFosse

This simple wing is an agile sprite. Toss it high into the air, any way that you can, and it will loop, dart and glide to a graceful finish. This wing is stackable. Richard Alexander named this design "Stacked Over Logan" because it reminded him of traffic flying over his home in Nahant, Massachusetts: a peninsula in the vicinity of Boston's Logan Airport. During busy periods, planes waiting for their turn to land are assigned holding patterns at different altitudes, called "stacking." When you toss a stacked handful of these models, the confusing burst of planes may seem chaotic, but they never collide! So, fold a colorful squadron of at least a half dozen planes for each hand, and toss them all into the air. The explosion of color and action may remind you of fireworks!

Use squares of paper approximately 6 inches (15 cm). Colorful origami paper is great to use, if you have it. Consider using colorful magazine pages, old calendar pages and even junk mail—it's a fun way to recycle!

Square

6 inches
or
15 cm

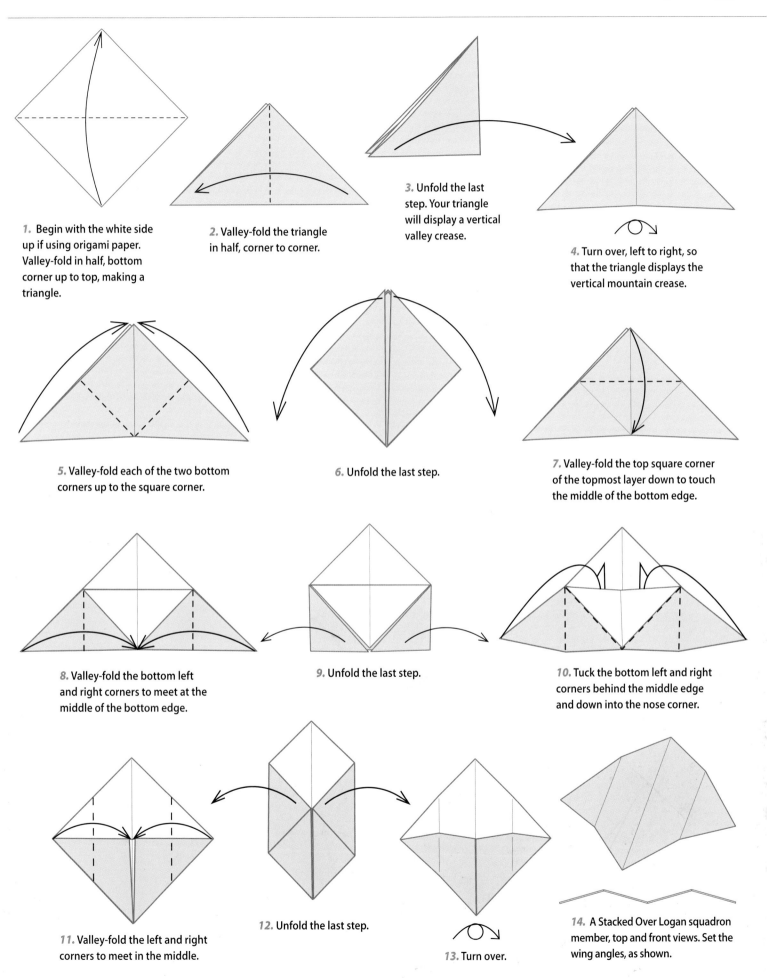

1. Begin with the white side up if using origami paper. Valley-fold in half, bottom corner up to top, making a triangle.

2. Valley-fold the triangle in half, corner to corner.

3. Unfold the last step. Your triangle will display a vertical valley crease.

4. Turn over, left to right, so that the triangle displays the vertical mountain crease.

5. Valley-fold each of the two bottom corners up to the square corner.

6. Unfold the last step.

7. Valley-fold the top square corner of the topmost layer down to touch the middle of the bottom edge.

8. Valley-fold the bottom left and right corners to meet at the middle of the bottom edge.

9. Unfold the last step.

10. Tuck the bottom left and right corners behind the middle edge and down into the nose corner.

11. Valley-fold the left and right corners to meet in the middle.

12. Unfold the last step.

13. Turn over.

14. A Stacked Over Logan squadron member, top and front views. Set the wing angles, as shown.

AIRPLANE #2
THE CHUCK FINN

By Michael G. LaFosse

Here is another simple wing that performs extremely well. This one sports relatively large vertical stabilizers, which keep it on track during flight. While the Stacked Over Logan wing has a delightful, erratic flight pattern, the Chuck Finn has a more stable glide.

No matter how you manage to get this wing into the air, it will right itself and glide gracefully, but try these two different launch styles for the Chuck Finn. Style one is to simply hold the model at the middle of the back edge and raise it high above your head. Give the plane the slightest push forward as you let go. It will glide long and true. This launch works well from an elevated location. The other launch style makes it loop! Hold the model by the nose corner, with the fins pointing toward you and the back of your hand facing up. Move your arm swiftly upward and let go, launching the plane nose first toward the sky. It will soar upward, loop, and then gracefully glide to a gentle landing.

Choose squares from 6 inches (15 cm) to 10 inches (25 cm).

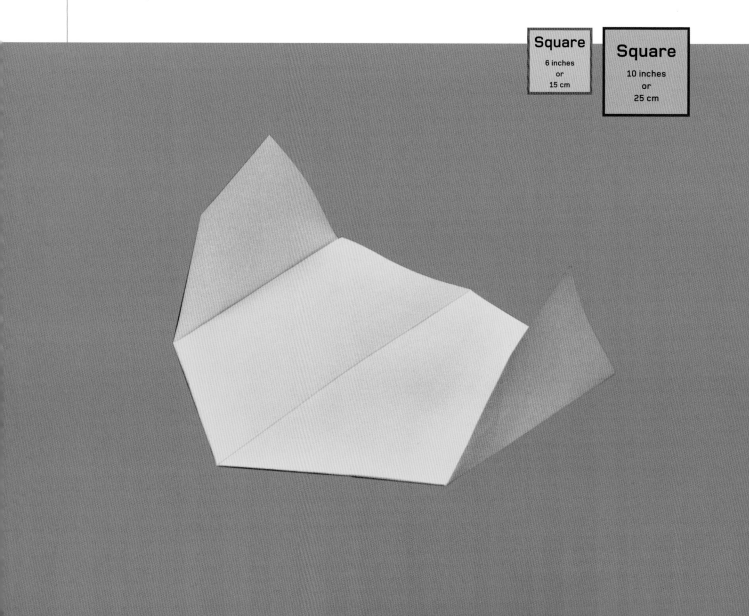

Square

6 inches
or
15 cm

Square

10 inches
or
25 cm

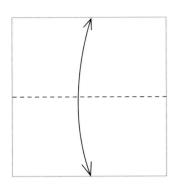

1. Begin with the white side up if using origami paper. Valley-fold in half, bottom edge up to the top edge, making a rectangle. Unfold.

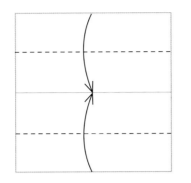

2. Valley-fold the bottom and top edges to the middle crease, forming upper and lower rectangular flaps.

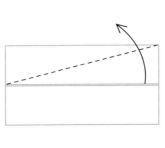

3. Diagonally valley-fold the upper rectangular flap in half by moving the bottom right corner of the flap above the top edge of the paper.

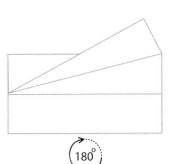

4. Your paper should look like this. Rotate the model 180 degrees.

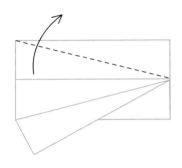

5. Diagonally fold the upper rectangular flap in half by moving the bottom left corner of the flap above the top edge of the paper.

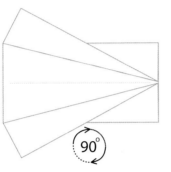

6. Your paper should look like this. Rotate the model 90 degrees clockwise.

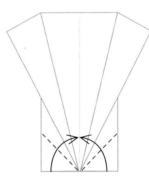

7. Valley-fold the two bottom corners up to meet at the vertical center crease, forming a triangle at the bottom.

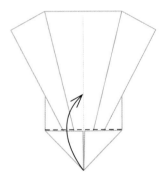

8. Valley-fold up along the triangle's top edge, making it point upward.

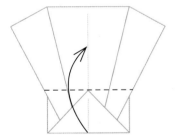

9. Valley-fold up along the level where the triangle's top corner touches the paper, forming a rectangular area in front.

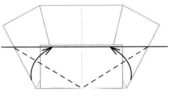

10. Valley-fold each half of the bottom edge of the rectangle up, forming two triangular flaps and a pointed nose. Notice that the top edges of the triangular flaps must be horizontal and that they must not move beyond the top edge of the rectangle, indicated by the red line.

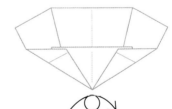

11. Your model will look like this. Turn over, left to right.

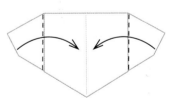

12. Valley-fold the indicated side flaps tightly over the vertical folded edges, forming the fins.

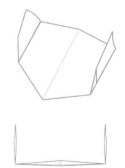

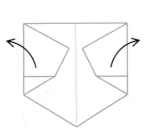

13. Stand the two fins up, 90 degrees from the body of the wing.

14. The Chuck Finn, top and front views.

AIRPLANE #3
THE FINGER WINGER

By Michael G. LaFosse

Square
6 inches
or
15 cm

Square
10 inches
or
25 cm

This wing is interesting to fold, and it is a great flyer. It can be launched the same way as the Chuck Finn, but I designed it to be launched off the end of your index finger! Simply insert your finger into the nose from underneath and snap your arm forward. The plane will dart away from your hand and often loop around. Try launching this plane straight forward, up, down, or even sideways.

Use squares from 6 inches (15 cm) to 10 inches (25 cm).

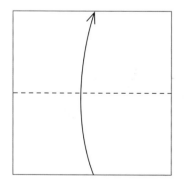

1. Begin with the white side up if using origami paper. Valley-fold in half, bottom edge up to the top edge, making a rectangle.

2. Be sure that the folded edge is at the bottom of the shape. Fold only the short, right edge in half, making a short crease that marks the halfway level of the paper. Return the folded edge to the bottom.

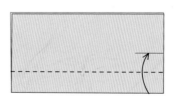

3. Valley-fold the bottom folded edge up to the level of the crease.

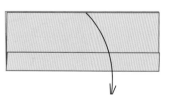

4. Open the paper completely.

5. Look carefully at the creases on the inside of the paper. The center crease is a valley crease. The outer creases are a mountain crease and a valley crease. Reverse the outer valley crease, making it a mountain crease. Look ahead at diagram 6.

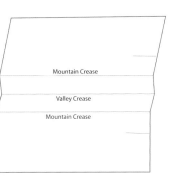

6. The crease pattern should now be mountain, valley, and mountain.

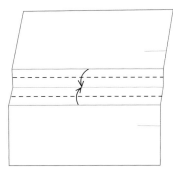

7. One at a time, carefully fold each mountain crease to meet at the center valley crease.

8. Your paper should look like this. Notice the short creases to the right. Rotate the paper so that these creases are at the bottom. This will ensure that the trailing edge of the model will be clean and flat.

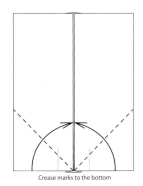

9. Valley-fold each of the two bottom edges to meet at the vertical split in the middle, forming two triangle flaps.

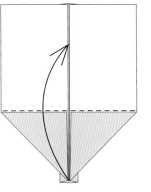

10. Valley-fold the paper up at the level of the top edges of the triangle flaps.

11. Valley-fold each of the two new bottom edges to meet at the vertical center of the paper. Notice that a portion of the paper must travel behind the vertical paper bar to do this. Look ahead at the diagram for Step 12.

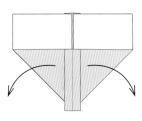

12. Return the two edges to the bottom.

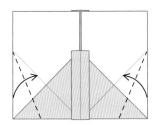

13. Valley-fold the left and right edges to the nearby creases.

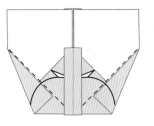

14. Using the existing creases, valley-fold the narrow triangle flaps up and over, forming the leading edges of the wings.

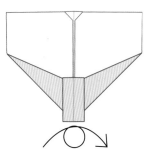

15. Mountain-fold the center tab down inside the model, as far as it will go. Mountain-fold in the top two corners at the top of the split. This last step will lock the back layers flat and decrease drag.

16. Your paper should look like this. Turn over.

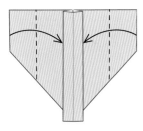

17. Form the vertical stabilizers by valley-folding the left and right edges inward to the indicated folded edges.

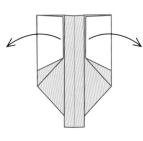

18. Move the flaps outward and make them stand perpendicular to the main body of the model.

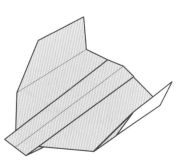

19. The Finger Winger.

AIRPLANE #4
THE ART-DECO WING

By Michael G. LaFosse

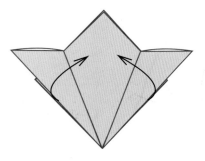

Square
6 inches
or
15 cm

Square
10 inches
or
25 cm

This wing is my favorite because it embodies all of the elements I consider essential to good design. In 1975, while I was studying at the University of Tampa, I designed this model and dropped it from my dorm window. The warm, rising Florida breezes would gently carry this little wing for blocks! It glides well no matter how you get this wing into the air, but I recommend two basic ways to launch the wing. My first recommended launch method: Hold it from behind, in the middle, just behind the nose, and raise it high above your head. Release it with the slightest push. It will glide long and true. The other way I like to launch it will make it loop: Hold the model by the front of the nose, with the little fins pointing toward you and the back of your hand facing up. Move your arm swiftly up and then let go, launching the plane nose-first toward the sky. It will soar, loop, and gracefully glide a good distance. It has a long glide ratio. Try stacking several wings and launching them all at once!

The best paper size is approximately 6 inches or 15 72 square; up to 10 inches or 25 cm square.

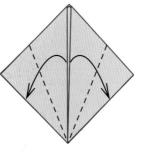

1. Begin with the white side up if using origami paper. Valley-fold in half, bottom corner up to top, making a triangle.

2. Valley-fold the bottom corners to match the top corner.

3. Valley-fold the indicated edges to match the outer edges of the paper.

4. Return the edges to the center.

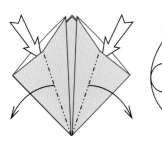

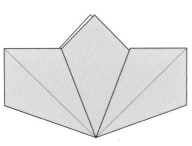

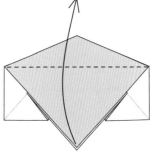

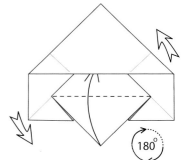

5. Open the layers of each of the two triangle flaps, like a cone. Flatten into kite shapes. Look ahead at diagram 6.

6. Turn the paper over, top to bottom.

7. Valley-fold the large flap up.

8. Valley-fold the indicated flap up and tuck it inside the paper. Rotate the model 180 degrees.

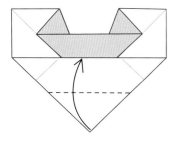

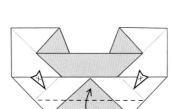

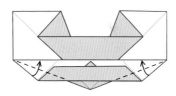

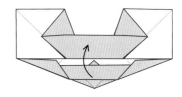

9. Valley-fold the corner of the bottom flap up to touch the middle of the folded edge, above.

10. Valley-fold the bottom edge up. Keep this flap within the creases, indicated by "X" marks in the diagram.

11. Valley-fold the left and right side flaps up to the folded edge.

12. Flip the main flap up.

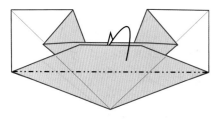

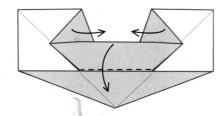

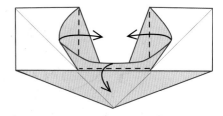

13. Mountain-fold the flap inside the model.

14. Valley-fold the middle edge down tightly against the top edge of the triangular nose area. Push the indicated corners inward to open the paper for squash folding.

15. Continue to move the middle edge downward while pushing the side corners inward and down to flatten. Look ahead at the next diagram.

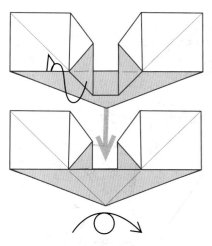

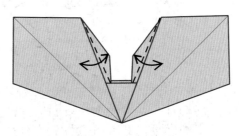

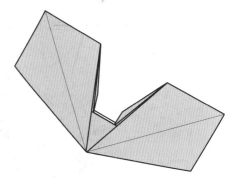

16. Tuck the flattened flap inside the model. Turn over.

17. Valley-fold the indicated flaps tightly over the back edges of the wings; then stand them vertically away from the wings. These are the vertical stabilizers.

18. The Art-Deco Wing. Launch it high overhead. Just about any way you get it into the air will get it to glide. Experiment with different papers; different sizes, too!

AIRPLANE #5
THE SHUTTLE DART

By Michael G. LaFosse

This little glider reminds me of various shuttlecraft from sci-fi television shows and movies. Despite its simplicity, I took many years to perfect it. Though I have published earlier versions of this model as early as 1995, it was in the first version that I discovered a new type of nose lock for gliders. Upon preparing this book I reinvestigated the design and I was able to make a significant improvement in its reliability and performance, and so this book has the first diagrams showing the perfected model. The new improvements are in steps 2 through 4, yielding a different proportion. I also made a final determination about the style of elevons, and together, these refinements make this version more interesting to fold and more reliable to fly. I launch the Shuttle Dart with a gentle push.

The best size squares are from 6 inches (15 cm), up to 10 inches (25 cm).

Square
6 inches
or
15 cm

Square
10 inches
or
25 cm

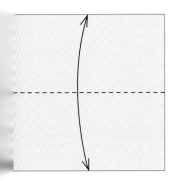

1. Begin with colored side up if using origami paper. Valley-fold in half, bottom edge up to the top edge, making a rectangle. Unfold.

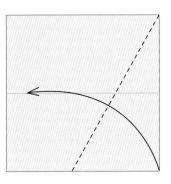

2. Valley-fold the lower right corner to the horizontal crease, while ensuring that the fold reaches the top right corner.

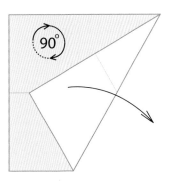

3. Unfold and rotate the paper 90 degrees clockwise, so that the center crease is vertical and the high end of the slanted crease is to the left.

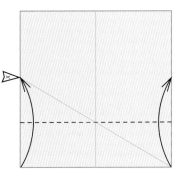

4. Valley-fold the bottom edge up to the level of the high end of the slanted crease, indicated by the "X."

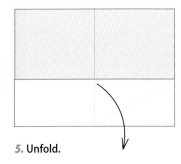

5. Unfold.

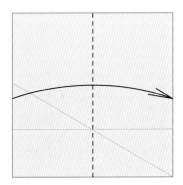

6. Valley-fold the paper in half, left edge to right, using the vertical center crease.

7. Notice the crease pattern at the bottom. Valley-fold the lower left-side folded edge up to the horizontal crease, forming a right-triangle flap.

8. Valley-fold the right edge of the triangle flap to the long, left edge (hypotenuse). This step forms the creases for the nose lock.

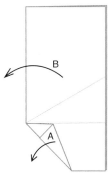

9. (A) Unfold the paper at the bottom. (B) Open the paper completely.

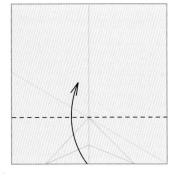

10. Use the existing horizontal crease to Valley-fold the bottom edge up.

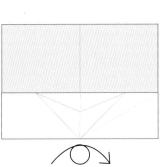

11. Turn the paper over, left to right.

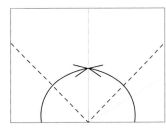

12. The folded edge should be at the bottom. Valley-fold the left and the right halves of the bottom folded edge to meet at the middle crease.

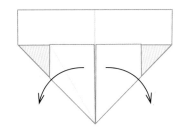

13. Bring the corners back down to the bottom.

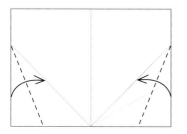

14. Valley-fold the left and the right edges to the 45-degree creases.

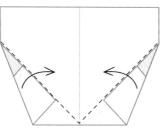

15. Use the 45-degree crease to Valley-fold the indicated flaps up, forming a pointed nose.

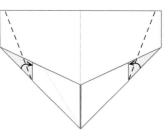

16. Valley-fold the Indicated edge of the wing to match the nearby vertical edge of paper, forming the fins.

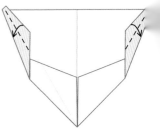

17. Valley-fold the long cut edge of each fin to match the long folded edge. This will add horizontal flaps to the fins.

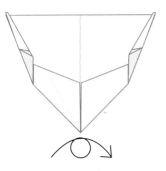

18. Turn over, left to right.

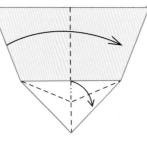

19. Valley-fold the model in half while moving the free edge of the triangle of paper down toward the nose. The existing creases will allow you to do this easily. This will form the nose lock.

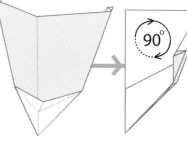

20. Folding in progress. Rotate the model 90 degrees clockwise.

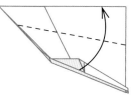

21. Valley-fold the long edge of the wing up to match the top edge of the paper.

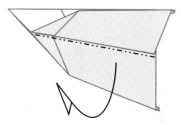

22. Fold the other wing to match on the other side.

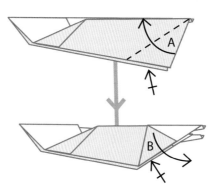

23. Folding the elevons: (A) Valley-fold the back edge of the wing to match the leading edge. Repeat behind on the other wing. (B) Unfold.

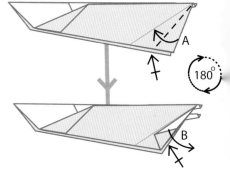

24. (A) Valley-fold the back edge of the wing to the crease. Repeat behind on the other wing. (B) Unfold. You now have adjustable elevons. Smooth the flap flat: a little flap goes a long way. You can adjust the flaps to make the plane loop, turn left or right, or for level flight. Rotate 180 degrees.

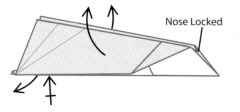

25. Open the wings straight out to the side. Open the fins to form a stair-step shape.

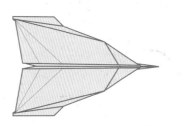

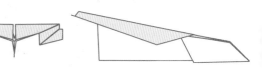

26. The Shuttle Dart.

AIRPLANE #6
THE ARROW

By Michael G. LaFosse

I have designed many planes from US letter paper (8 ½ by 11 inches). Not only is it handy, I find these proportions work great for models that are well balanced, resulting in good flight. Even when I design planes from squares—an origami penchant of mine—I sometimes begin by folding the squares to approximate the proportions of an 8 ½ by 11-inch sheet.

This model is one result; it is an adaptation of my Shuttle Dart (page 32). The remnant flaps, formed when 1/8th of the two opposite sides of the square are folded inward, provide paper for the vertical stabilizers. One bonus is the resulting arrow shape, even more evident when using duo paper (colored differently on each side).

Small to medium sized models fly best. Standard origami paper is excellent for this plane.

Use thin paper at least 6 inches square.

Square
6 inches
or
15 cm

Square
10 inches
or
25 cm

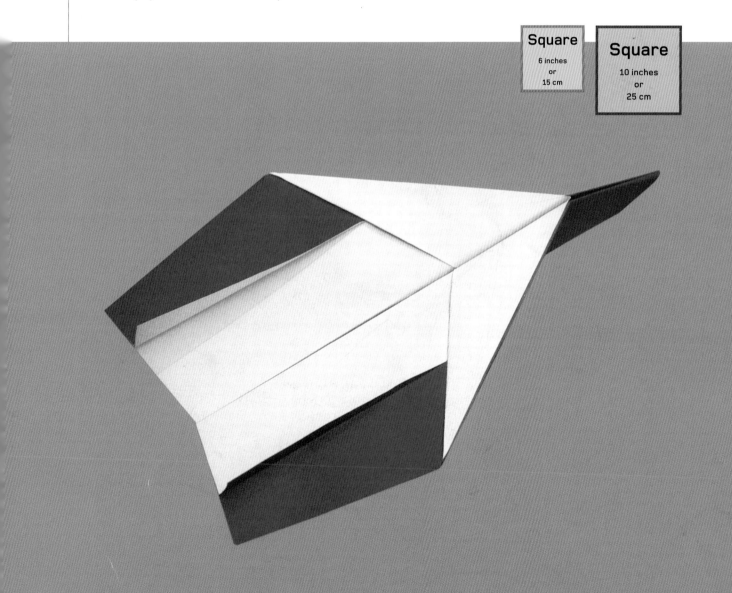

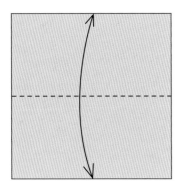

1. Begin with colored side up if using origami paper. Valley-fold in half, bottom edge up to top edge, making a rectangle. Unfold.

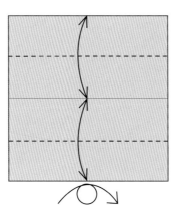

2. Valley-fold the bottom and top edges to the middle crease, forming upper and lower rectangular flaps. Unfold. Turn the paper over, left to right.

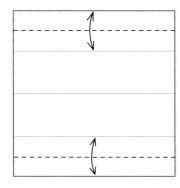

3. Valley-fold the top and bottom edges to the nearest crease. Unfold.

4. Valley-fold the top and bottom right-side corners to the nearest crease.

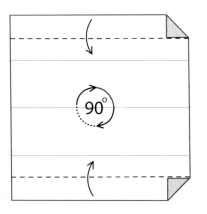

5. Use the topmost and bottommost creases to fold these edges over. Rotate 90 degrees clockwise, so that the beveled corners are at the bottom.

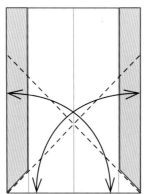

6. Valley-fold the bottom edge to the left edge and unfold. Fold the bottom edge to the right edge and unfold.

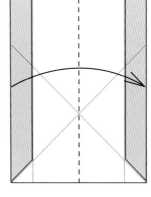

7. Valley-fold in half, left edge to right.

8. Valley-fold the bottom edge to the angled crease, forming a triangular flap.

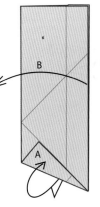

9. (A) Unfold the triangular flap and fold it around to the other side, making the crease flexible. You can flex it a few more times, which will make Step 16 easier. (B) Open.

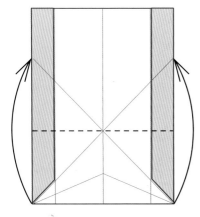

10. Valley-fold the bottom corners up to the top of the X-shaped creases.

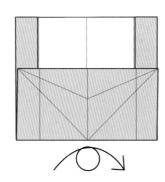

11. Turn the paper over, left to right, keeping the folded edge at the bottom.

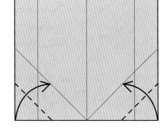

12. Valley-fold the bottom corners to the center of the angled creases. It will be helpful to not quite touch the crease with these corners.

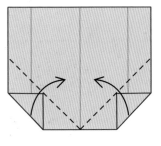

13. Using the angled creases, fold the bottom flaps up, forming trapezoids.

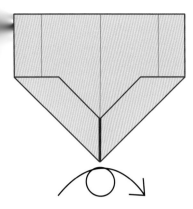

14. Turn the paper over.

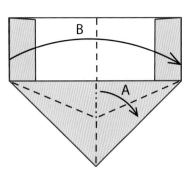

15. Fold the bottom corner to the intersection of the creases. (A) With the model folded slightly in half, pull the center of the top edge of the nose paper forward. Let the creases guide you in forming a V-shaped flap. (B) Fold the model in half. Look at diagram 16 for a progress view.

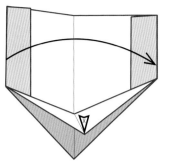

16. In progress. Fold completely in half, letting the V-shaped flap fold in half and move into the nose of the plane.

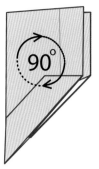

17. Your model should look like this. Rotate 90 degrees clockwise.

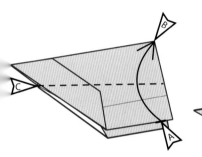

18. Fold the topmost layer up, forming one of the wings. For best angle, use these reference marks: Match wing edge "A" to tail corner "B," while guiding the left end of the crease to hit the nose at point "C."

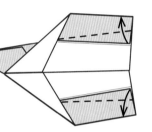

19. Your model should look like this. Form the vertical stabilizers by folding the indicated free corners to touch the outer wing edges.

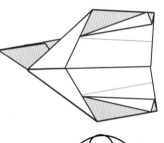

20. Your model should look like this. Turn over, left to right.

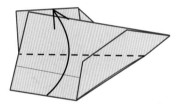

21. Fold the other wing up to match the first.

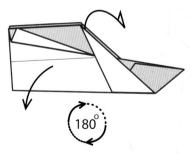

22. Your model should look like this. Open the wings out and rotate 180 degrees.

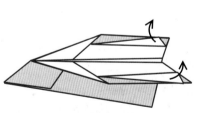

23. Stand the vertical stabilizers up.

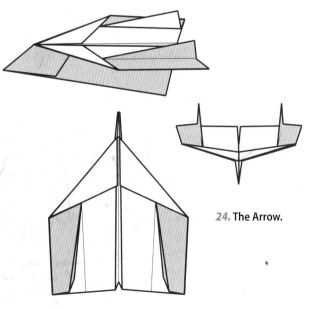

24. The Arrow.

AIRPLANE #7
THE RODNEY

By Michael G. LaFosse

It can be a challenge, trying to name new paper airplane designs. Nearly every book on paper planes has many of the same names such as "Saber" and "Stiletto," so I simply decided to call this one "Rodney." It is a good glider, and it can do loops if you throw it hard. This particular design has lots of potential for creative attention: Why not experiment with the fin shapes and wing angles? You may find yourself in a position to come up with an original name for your new plane!

Use paper that is anywhere from 6 to 10 inches, square.

Square
6 inches
or
15 cm

Square
10 inches
or
25 cm

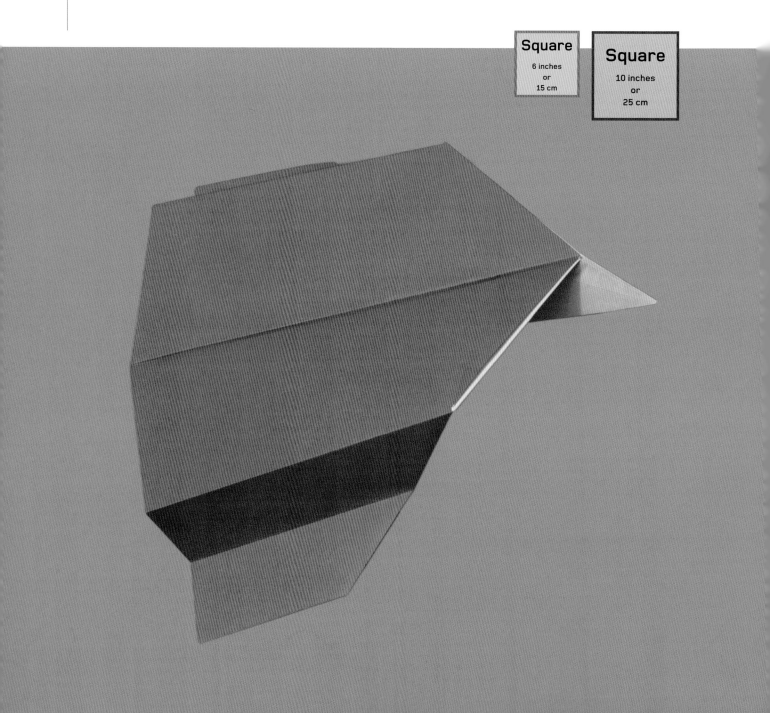

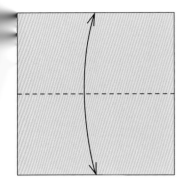

1. Begin with the colored side up if using origami paper. Valley-fold in half, bottom edge up to the top edge, making a rectangle. Unfold.

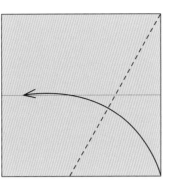

2. Valley-fold the lower right corner to the horizontal crease while ensuring that the fold reaches the top right corner.

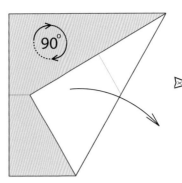

3. Unfold and rotate the paper 90 degrees clockwise, so that the center crease is vertical and the high end of the slanted crease is to the left.

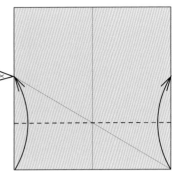

4. Valley-fold the bottom edge up to the level of the high end of the slanted crease, indicated by the "X."

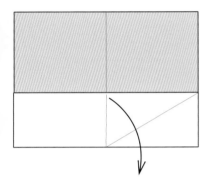

5. Unfold.

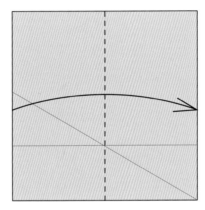

6. Valley-fold the paper in half, left edge to right, using the vertical center crease.

7. Notice the crease pattern at the bottom. Valley-fold the lower left-side folded edge up to the horizontal crease, forming a right-triangle flap.

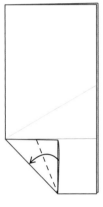

8. Valley-fold the right edge of the triangle flap to the long, left edge (hypotenuse). This step forms the creases for the nose lock.

9. Valley-fold both layers of the bottom right corner over so that the fold runs between the horizontal crease and the bottom point of the nose lock fold.

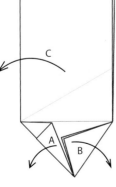

10. (A and B) Unfold the paper at the bottom. (C) Open the paper completely.

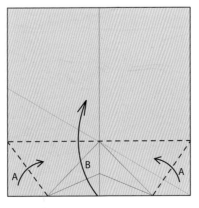

11. Use the existing horizontal creases, (A) valley-fold the bottom left and right corners over and (B) valley-fold the bottom edge up.

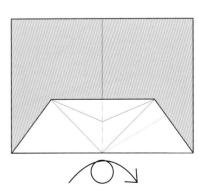

12. Turn the paper over, left to right.

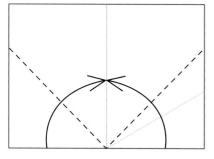

13. The folded edge should be at the bottom. Valley-fold the left and the right halves of the bottom folded edge to meet at the middle crease.

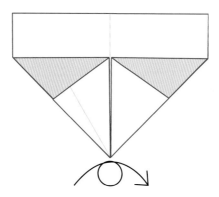

14. Turn the paper over, left to right.

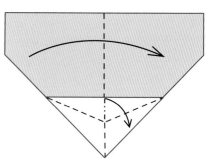

15. Valley-fold the model in half while moving the free edge of the triangle of paper down toward the nose. The existing creases will allow you to do this easily. This will form the nose lock.

16. Folding in progress. When the fold is completed, rotate the model 90 degrees clockwise.

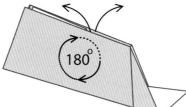

17. Valley-fold the top layer up to form a wing. Make the fold span between the nose lock and the back corner, marked with "X"s.

18. Turn the paper over, left to right.

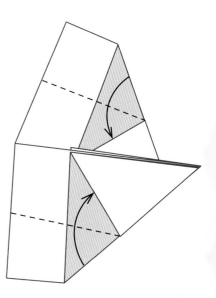

19. Valley-fold the wings in. Match the leading edges to the angled, multi-layer nose paper for alignment.

20. Valley-fold the wing edges to the outermost folded edges, forming the fins.

21. Valley-fold the lower wing up to match the one above.

22. Rotate the model 180 degrees to make it upright. Open out the wings and the fins.

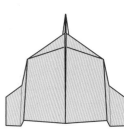

23. The Rodney. The wings should be set at a slight *dihedral* ("Y" shape), and the fins opened to make a stair-step shape.

AIRPLANE #8
THE STORMIN' NORMAN

By Michael G. LaFosse

My uncle Norman introduced me to paper airplanes the summer before I began Kindergarten. Norman is my dad's youngest brother, and he spent hours teaching my brother and me how to fold and fly a wonderful, wide-winged paper airplane that easily did large loops like the acrobatic "barnstormers" that I had seen on television. Because I would lose the plane almost immediately, I would go back to him and watch him fold another, over and over, until I had memorized it. When I designed this plane I recalled those long-gone days of simple fun.

Launch this plane with a gentle throw and it will glide beautifully. A harder launch will make it loop. You can experiment with different fin configurations on the wings to get it to do even more stunts.

Use squares between 6 and 10 inches.

Square
6 inches
or
15 cm

Square
10 inches
or
25 cm

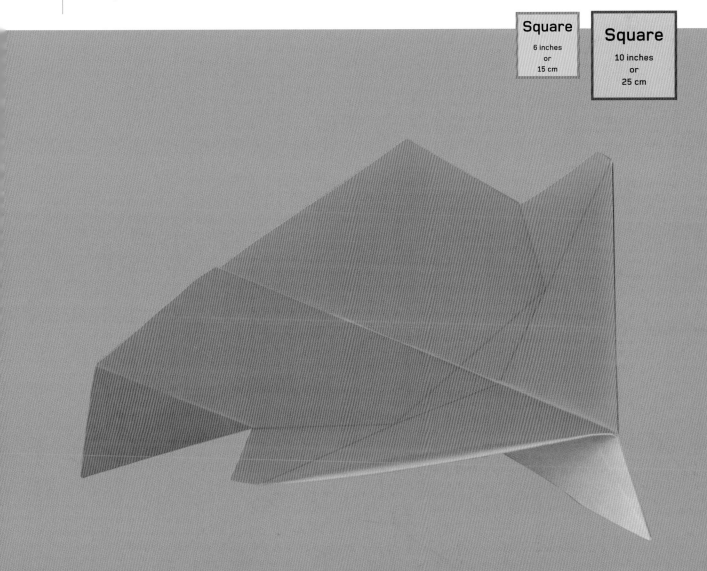

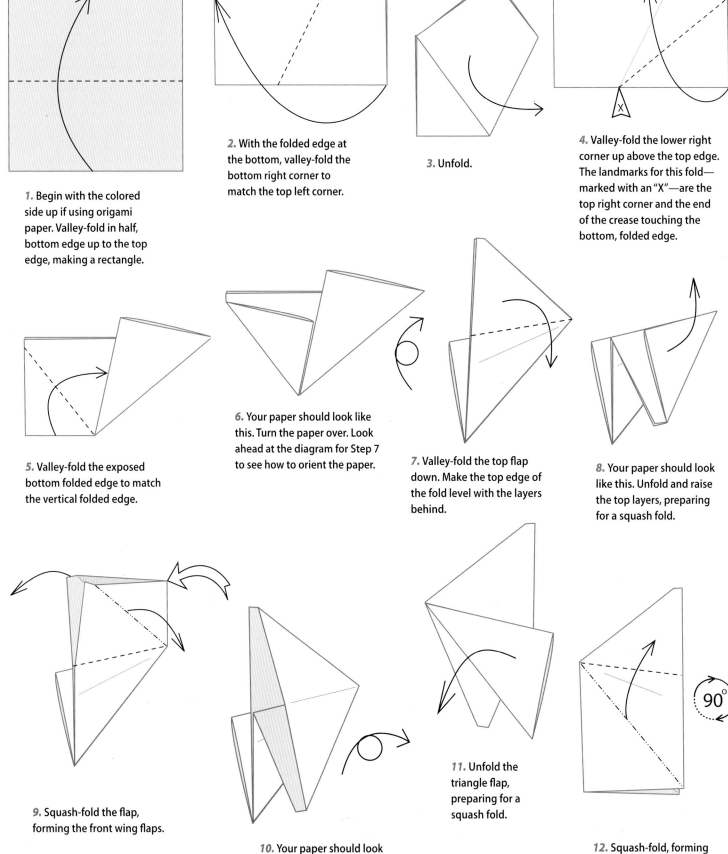

1. Begin with the colored side up if using origami paper. Valley-fold in half, bottom edge up to the top edge, making a rectangle.

2. With the folded edge at the bottom, valley-fold the bottom right corner to match the top left corner.

3. Unfold.

4. Valley-fold the lower right corner up above the top edge. The landmarks for this fold—marked with an "X"—are the top right corner and the end of the crease touching the bottom, folded edge.

5. Valley-fold the exposed bottom folded edge to match the vertical folded edge.

6. Your paper should look like this. Turn the paper over. Look ahead at the diagram for Step 7 to see how to orient the paper.

7. Valley-fold the top flap down. Make the top edge of the fold level with the layers behind.

8. Your paper should look like this. Unfold and raise the top layers, preparing for a squash fold.

9. Squash-fold the flap, forming the front wing flaps.

10. Your paper should look like this. Turn the paper over, left to right.

11. Unfold the triangle flap, preparing for a squash fold.

12. Squash-fold, forming a triangle. Rotate 90 degrees clockwise.

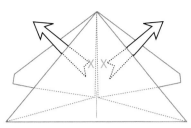

13. Your paper should look like this. Pull out the layers from between the front wing flaps and the tail flaps. Follow the "X"s to see where these edges belong. The model will not lie flat.

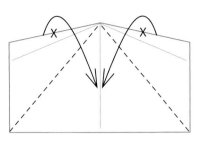

14. Valley-fold the top edges to meet at the middle crease.

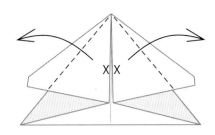

15. Return the "X" edges to their upper position.

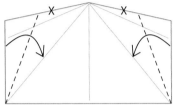

16. Valley-fold the left and the right edges to meet at the diagonal creases.

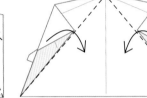

17. Valley-fold the left and the right edges to meet at the center crease.

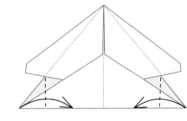

18. Valley-fold the tail corners straight in, aligning the bottom edges together.

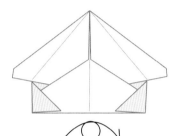

19. Turn the paper over, left to right.

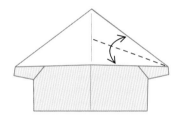

20. Install pre-creases for the nose lock by folding the top edge of the upper triangle area to the bottom right edge of the triangle. You only need to crease through to the center from each side.

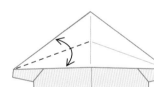

21. Repeat this fold on the left side of the triangle.

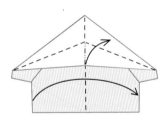

22. Form the nose lock by folding the model in half while moving the bottom edge of the paper triangle upward, into the nose.

23. Nose lock in progress.

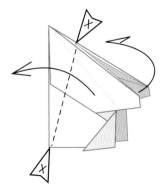

24. Fold the wings tightly over the body of the plane. Notice the landmarks, marked "X," for the angle of these folds.

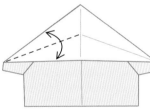

25. Open the wings and set the tail fins.

26. The Stormin' Norman. Notice that the wings should be set at a slight *dihedral* ("Y" shape). Launch the plane swiftly and at an upward angle for loops and a longer flight; gently forward for slow, graceful glides.

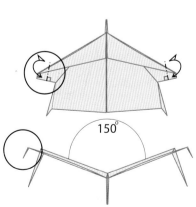

27. The Stormin' Norman with wing fins added.

AIRPLANE #9
THE FLYING FOX

By Michael G. LaFosse

My interest in designing new origami planes has its seasons. It usually begins in early autumn, as the weather in New England at that time is most comfortable for me. It entices me to spend more time outdoors; and I enjoy the smells and the rattling sounds of the dry leaves. I will sit in a quiet spot, where I can see the trees and the water, and I will begin to fold, automatically at first, as if relying upon muscle memory to get a good start. Perhaps it is the many years of persistent investigation that is at work here, but new designs begin to appear spontaneously; and then I will be up in a flash, test-flying, measuring the results, and making changes. The Flying Fox came to me in this way; but it seemed to fold itself—clever as a fox—and it was an elegant design from the beginning. A blunt-nose version is a nice variation: Fold the nose point in a bit, at Step 22, just before folding the model in half. This modification will increase the flight distance. It is an interesting place in this design to experiment, critique, and then make measured changes.

Use paper in size that is anywhere from 6 to 10 inches, square.

Square
6 inches
or
15 cm

Square
10 inches
or
25 cm

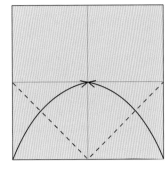

1. Begin with the colored side up if using origami paper. Valley-fold in half, edge to edge, both ways. Unfold after each.

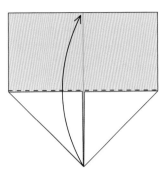

2. Valley-fold the bottom two corners to meet at the middle where the creases cross.

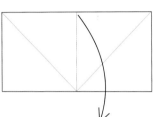

3. Valley-fold the bottom corner up to the middle of the top edge.

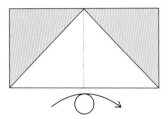

4. Turn the paper over, left to right, keeping the folded edge at the bottom.

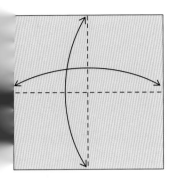

5. Valley-fold the bottom two corners up to meet at the middle of the top edge.

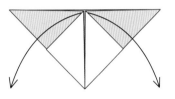

6. Return the corners to the bottom.

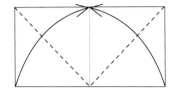

7. Move the front flap down.

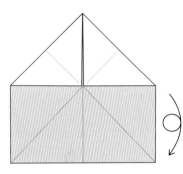

8. Turn the paper over, top to bottom.

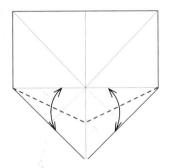

9. Notice that the bottom half of the paper is in the shape of a triangle. One at a time, valley-fold the bottom left and the bottom right edges of the triangle to the top edge of the triangle. You only need to crease through to the center from each side.

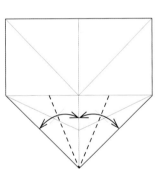

10. One at a time, valley-fold the bottom left and the bottom right edges of the triangle to the vertical center crease of the triangle. In each fold, you only need to crease from the bottom corner up to the top edge of the triangle.

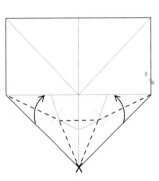

11. Simultaneously fold the left and the right edges of the triangle to the top edge. The bottom corner, marked with an "X," will stand up, forming an open pyramid.

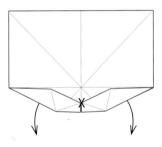

12. Loosen the layers of paper that are underneath the model and fold them out where they can be seen. You may need to let the layers open freely to start. You can then move the layers back together.

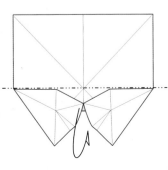

13. Use the horizontal crease to mountain-fold the lower folds to the underside of the upper rectangle flap. You will need to do this off the table.

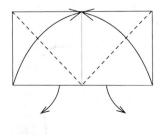

14. Valley-fold the bottom two corners of the rectangle to meet at the middle of the top edge, allowing the back-side layers to come over to the top side. You will be able to flatten the model on the table in the shape represented by Step 15's diagram.

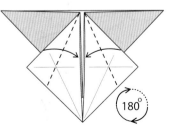

15. Valley-fold the top two edges of the square-diamond area to meet at the middle. Rotate the paper 180 degrees.

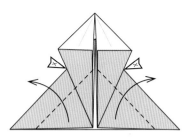

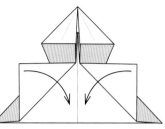

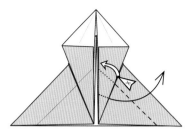

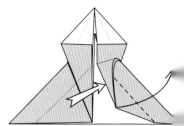

16. Prepare for making the wings by folding out the two corners that are to be found at the middle of the bottom edge. Valley-fold these corners out to form right-angle triangles, whose top edges will intersect the V-notches, indicated by the "X" pointers. Look at Step 17's diagram for the shape.

17. Return the triangle flaps to the bottom.

18. Open the space indicated by the "X" pointer by lifting both of the layers there. Inside-reverse-fold the wing through this open area.

19. The fold in progress. Use the guiding creases from Step 16 to place the angle correctly.

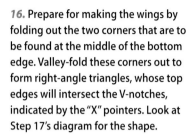

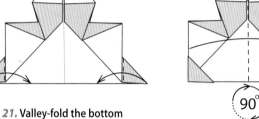

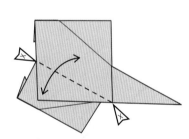

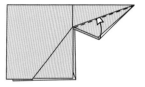

20. Flatten the wing. Repeat on the other side.

21. Valley-fold the bottom corner flaps squarely over the back of each wing.

22. Valley-fold in half and rotate 90 degrees clockwise.

23. Form the nose lock by tucking both layers of the indicated paper tightly into the nose.

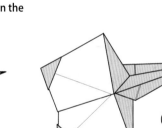

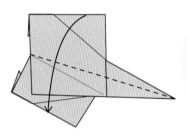

24. Valley-fold the top layer up to form a wing. Use the limit of the rear locking point of the nose lock to set the angle.

25. Your model should look like this. Turn over top to bottom.

26. Prepare for an inside-reverse fold of the vertical tail by folding the back corner flap up. Use the V-notch at the back of the wings and the beginning of the thick end of the fuselage as guides for the shape. Unfold.

27. Valley-fold the top wing down to match the wing underneath.

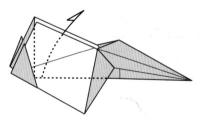

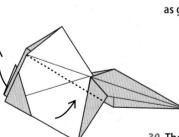

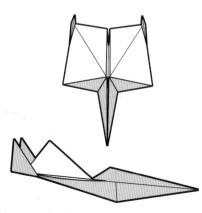

28. Inside-reverse-fold the vertical tail up in between the wings. Your pre-creases from Step 26 should make this step move easily.

29. Set the wings straight out to the sides and stand the wing flaps upright.

30. The Flying Fox. You can make a snub-nose version by folding the tip of the nose in at Step 22, just before folding the model in half. The snub-nose version can be thrown farther and with more force.

AIRPLANE #10
THE F-102 DELTA JET

By Michael G. LaFosse

My father was a photographer in the US Air Force, based in Roswell, NM, from 1950. His service was over before I was born. When I was a boy, he used to show me some of his photographs of the different types of aircraft. Fast-forward to 1978 and with a renewed interest in photos of the older planes, such as the F-102 fighter jet, I began to design replica origami delta wing models that would display satisfying detail, yet still fly well.

I made many primitive trials, which revealed its form-and-function issues clearly: putting the fuselage above the plane of the wings, as in the real aircraft, made the model top-heavy and it would flip over in flight. The tail originally needed tape to keep it closed—you still see this in the majority of models that use this origami style today—I didn't like that, and worked on solving it. Also, there was not enough weight in the front to enable the model to sufficiently accelerate forward.

Eventually I did find the right balance of weight, elevon control, and a wonderful way to lock the back without tape or glue… and it even flies well!

This model is a folding challenge for beginners, so hone your folding skills before attempting it. Launching it is a surprise to many: Since there is no descending throwing tab you actually hold one of the wings. Throw it like a conventional dart; it will right itself and glide rather well.

Use a thin square of at least 10 inches (25 cm). Larger is better. Begin with the white side up when using origami paper.

Square

10 inches
or
25 cm

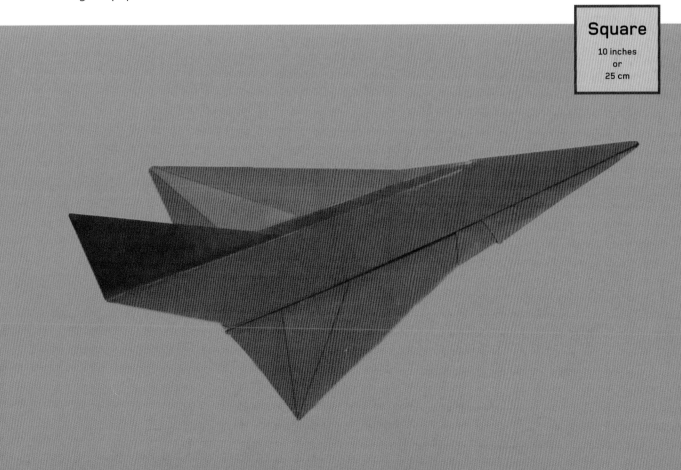

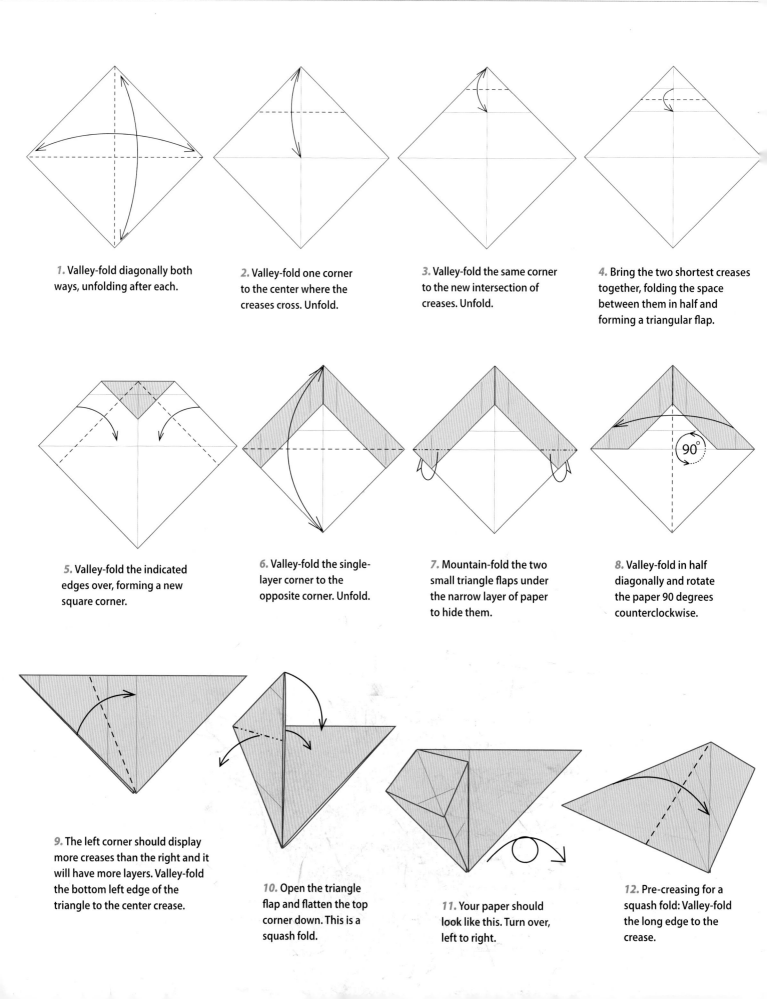

1. Valley-fold diagonally both ways, unfolding after each.

2. Valley-fold one corner to the center where the creases cross. Unfold.

3. Valley-fold the same corner to the new intersection of creases. Unfold.

4. Bring the two shortest creases together, folding the space between them in half and forming a triangular flap.

5. Valley-fold the indicated edges over, forming a new square corner.

6. Valley-fold the single-layer corner to the opposite corner. Unfold.

7. Mountain-fold the two small triangle flaps under the narrow layer of paper to hide them.

8. Valley-fold in half diagonally and rotate the paper 90 degrees counterclockwise.

9. The left corner should display more creases than the right and it will have more layers. Valley-fold the bottom left edge of the triangle to the center crease.

10. Open the triangle flap and flatten the top corner down. This is a squash fold.

11. Your paper should look like this. Turn over, left to right.

12. Pre-creasing for a squash fold: Valley-fold the long edge to the crease.

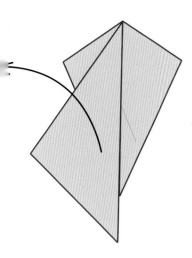

13. Unfold.

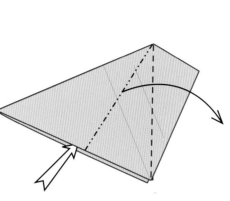

14. Open the triangle flap at the bottom edge and use the pre-crease to guide the symmetry of the squash fold.

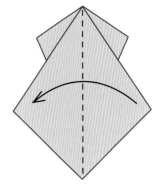

15. Your paper should look like this. Valley-fold the right half of the kite-shape to the left.

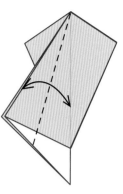

16. Pre-crease for a squash fold by valley-folding the long edge of the triangle flap to the crease. Unfold.

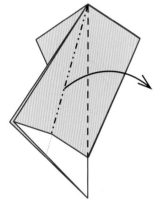

17. Squash-fold.

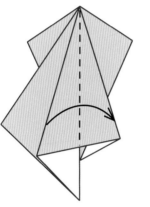

18. Valley-fold the left half of the squash to the right.

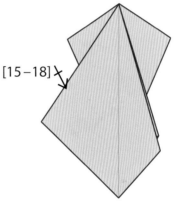

[15–18]

19. Repeat steps 15 through 18 on the left side of the model.

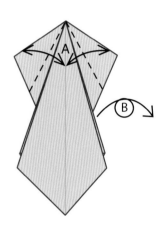

20. (A) Valley-fold the indicated edges to meet at the middle. Unfold. (B) Turn over, left to right.

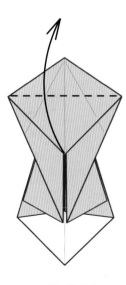

21. Valley-fold the top flap up.

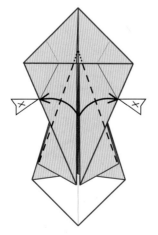

22. Pre-crease for the wings: Valley-fold each wing out so that their leading edges intersect the ends of the creases, marked with an "X." Be sure that the folds travel down to the bottom corner of each flap.

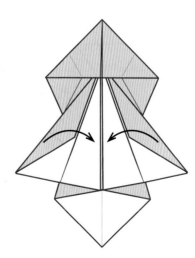

23. Your paper should look like this. Return the wings to the center.

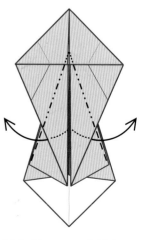

24. Inside-reverse-fold the wings by moving the inner valley crease out. Use your pre-creases to guide the shape.

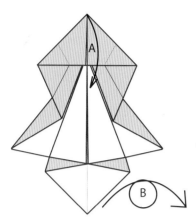

25. (A) Return the top flap down. (B) Turn over, left to right.

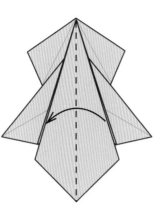

26. Your paper should look like this. Valley-fold the right half of the top layer to the left.

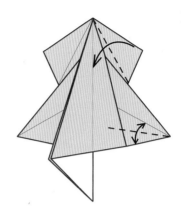

27. Fold the top right flap to the center crease. Form an elevator flap by valley-folding the back edge of the wing to the crease above it. Return the wing's edge to the back.

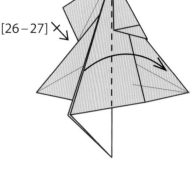

28. Repeat Steps 26 and 27 on the left side of the model.

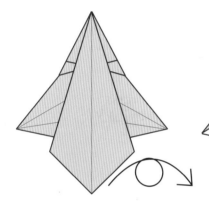

29. Turn over, left to right.

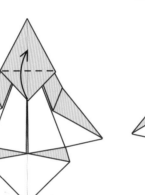

30. Valley-fold the indicated corner up.

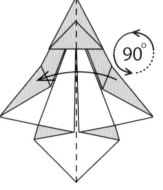

31. Valley-fold the model in half, wing-to-wing, and rotate 90 degrees counterclockwise.

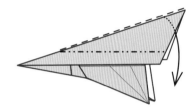

32. Inside-reverse-fold the back corner down below the fuselage (body of the plane). Make the mountain creases parallel to the bottom edge of the fuselage.

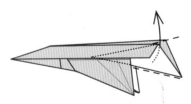

33. Inside-reverse-fold the same corner up to form the tail.

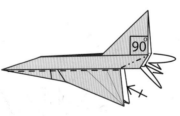

34. Make the angle between the back edge of the tail and the top edge of the fuselage 90 degrees. Mountain-fold the short, back edges of fuselage inside the model. Valley-fold the wings up.

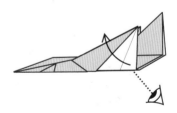

35. Open the underside by lifting the top half of the model.

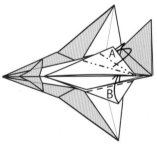

36. Make flap "A" narrow with two mountain folds. Tuck flap "B" under the base of flap A. This will lock the back end of the model.

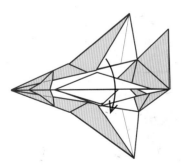

37. Close the fuselage and set the wings straight out to each side.

38. The F-102 Delta Jet. Launch the jet by holding onto one of the wings. This will necessitate that the plane be launched on its side, but it will quickly right itself and glide nicely.

AIRPLANE #11
THE F−14 TOMCAT

Designed by Michael G. LaFosse, text by Richard L. Alexander

Michael's first origami designs were paper airplanes, and this was the first model Michael published as "Aero-gami." It was also the first of his models that I videotaped to prove the point to Michael that video was an effective way to teach origami: after looking at the drawings and shaking my head, I mounted my video camera above Michael's folding table, and videotaped him folding the model. Without looking at the footage, I rewound the tape and loaned it to a neighbor who had an 8-year-old boy. Not only was he successful learning the model at his own pace, using the Pause and Play buttons on the video cassette player, he proceeded to take more origami lessons from us and even taught the models to his friends at school!

While trying to perfect an origami penguin in 1978, Michael came up with the base that became this fighter jet. He had been impressed by the F-14 when he saw a plastic hobby model in his local toy store. After perfecting the design over several years, he drew a set of diagrams with pen and ink, and lettered the instructions with a Kroy ribbon press-type machine. The booklets were featured in an ad he placed in *Popular Science*, and numerous photocopies circulated throughout the Air Force bases. We still hear from pilots and Air Force personnel about their experience folding and flying the F-14 Aero-gami model that Michael published in the early eighties.

Use paper at least 8 ½ inches, square. Begin with the white side up if using origami paper.

Square

10 inches
or
25 cm

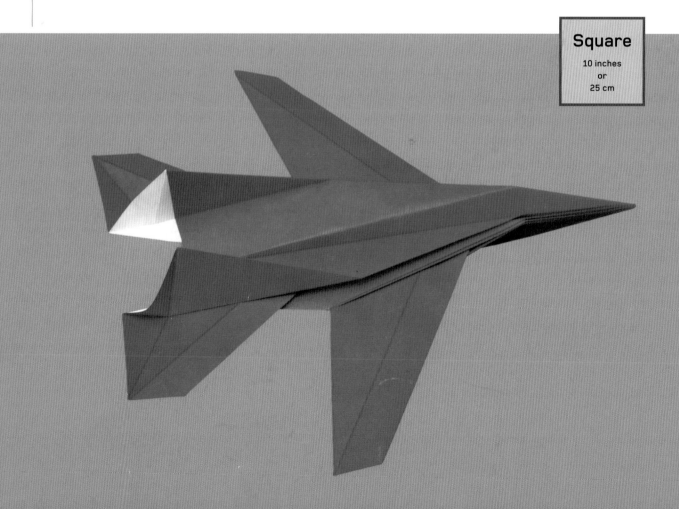

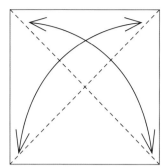

1. Valley-fold diagonally both ways, unfolding after each.

2. (A) Valley-fold the bottom edge to the center where the creases cross and make only a short crease. Unfold. (B) Make another short crease by valley-folding the bottom edge to the first short crease. Unfold. (C) Rotate the paper 90 degrees clockwise.

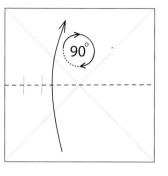

3. Valley-fold in half, bottom edge to top. Rotate the paper 90 degrees clockwise.

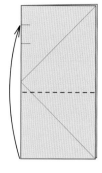

4. The short creases should now be near the top, along the folded edge. Valley-fold the bottom edge up to the top crease.

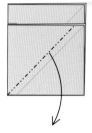

5. Your paper should look like this. Squash-fold the short half of the model.

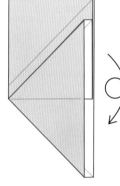

6. Turn the paper over, top to bottom.

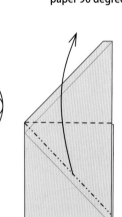

7. Squash-fold the rectangular bottom half of the model.

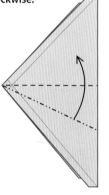

8. Your paper should now have four flaps. The larger flaps are topmost. Squash-fold one of the top flaps. Look ahead at the next drawing for the shape.

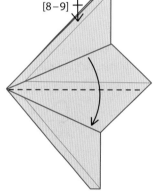

9. Valley-fold the top half of the squashed flap down. Repeat steps 8 and 9 on the other flap.

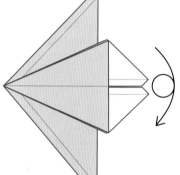

10. Turn the model over, top to bottom.

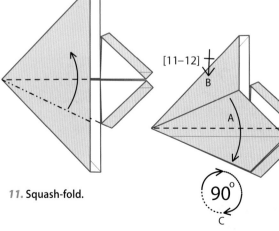

11. Squash-fold.

12. (A) Valley-fold the top half of the squashed flap down. (B) Repeat steps 11 and 12. (C) Rotate the model 90 degrees clockwise.

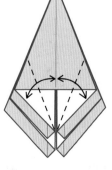

13. Valley-fold the short edges of the kite-shape to meet in the middle. Unfold.

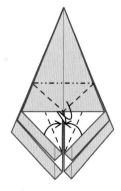

14. Mountain-fold the horizontal edge inside the model while re-folding the short kite edges to the middle.

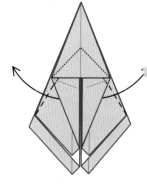

15. Your paper should look like this. Inside-reverse-fold the topmost flaps out to form the wings.

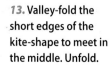

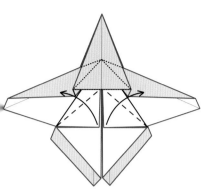

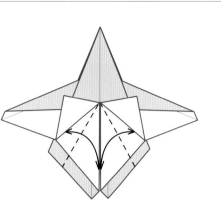

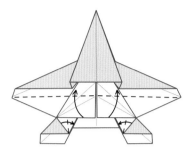

16. Valley-fold the indicated flaps out as far as they will go. Portions of the model will determine the limits.

17. Valley-fold the tail flaps out. Align the edges marked by the arrowheads. Return the flaps.

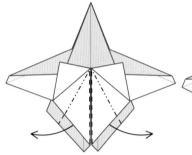

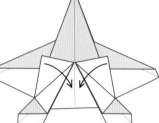

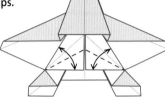

21. Valley-fold the bottom edges of the wings up. The creases should span from the tips of the wings to the tops of the crease formed in Step 20. Layers of paper below the wings will follow. Squash-fold these layers as the wings are flattened. Look ahead at drawing 22.

18. Inside-reverse-fold the tail flaps. Use the creases from Step 17 to guide the shape.

19. Return the indicated flaps to their original position.

20. Valley-fold the flaps. Align the edges marked by the arrowheads. Return the flaps.

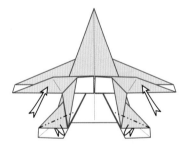

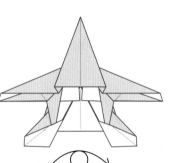

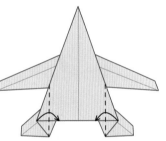

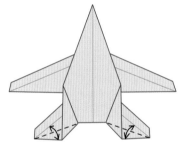

22. Tuck the loose edges of the wing paper under the leading edge flaps. Mountain-fold the flaps of the tails, making them trim.

23. Turn over, left to right.

24. Valley-fold the indicated flaps to form the twin vertical stabilizers. The creases should be parallel to the center crease.

25. Form the elevator flaps by folding the back edges of the tail to the tail creases. A bit of the vertical stabilizers will fold with them.

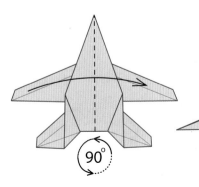

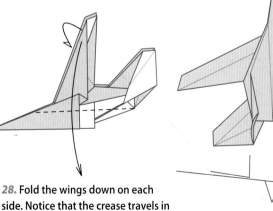

26. Valley-fold in half, wing-to-wing. Rotate 90 degrees counterclockwise.

27. Tuck the square-cornered flap under the tail paper, locking the back end.

28. Fold the wings down on each side. Notice that the crease travels in a line parallel to the bottom edge of the fuselage and that the crease ends at the top of the tail lock.

29. Set the wings with a slight *dihedral*. Raise the vertical stabilizers straight up. The F-14 Tomcat is ready!

AIRPLANE #12
THE SKY CRUISER

By Michael G. LaFosse

Here is an early design of mine, from the mid 1970s. This plane does not have nose or fuselage locks. Indeed, it flies better without them! I believe that some origami planes perform better when the fuselage is not held closed: these models may depend on the springy resilience of an open fuselage. My Pelican plane (page 67) is another example. It is important to remember to set the wings up in a "Y" shape, a *dihedral*, since the wings will level out as the fuselage opens in flight.

Take care to not launch the Sky Cruiser where bystanders or fragile objects could be struck, because it has a sharp, rigid nose. It is a terrific performer, and it can be launched gently indoors, or with great force outdoors.

Use 8 ½ by 11-inch US letter paper, or A4 letter paper.

US
Letter

A4

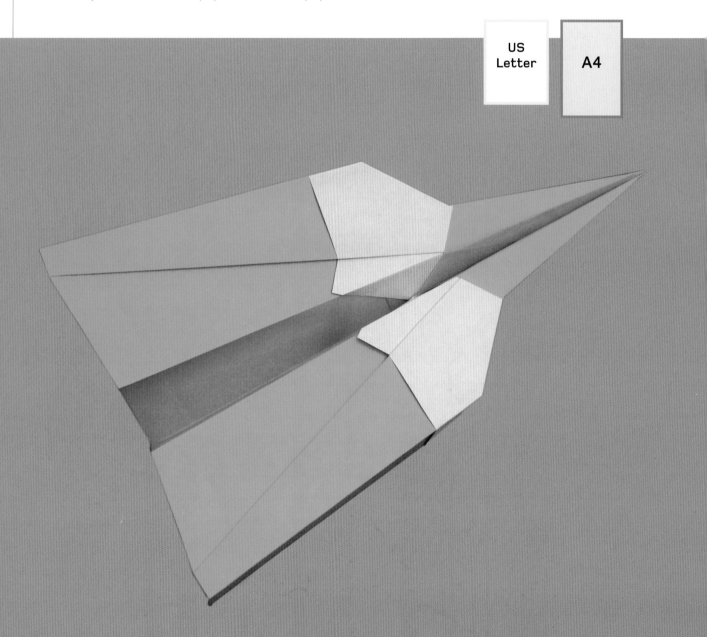

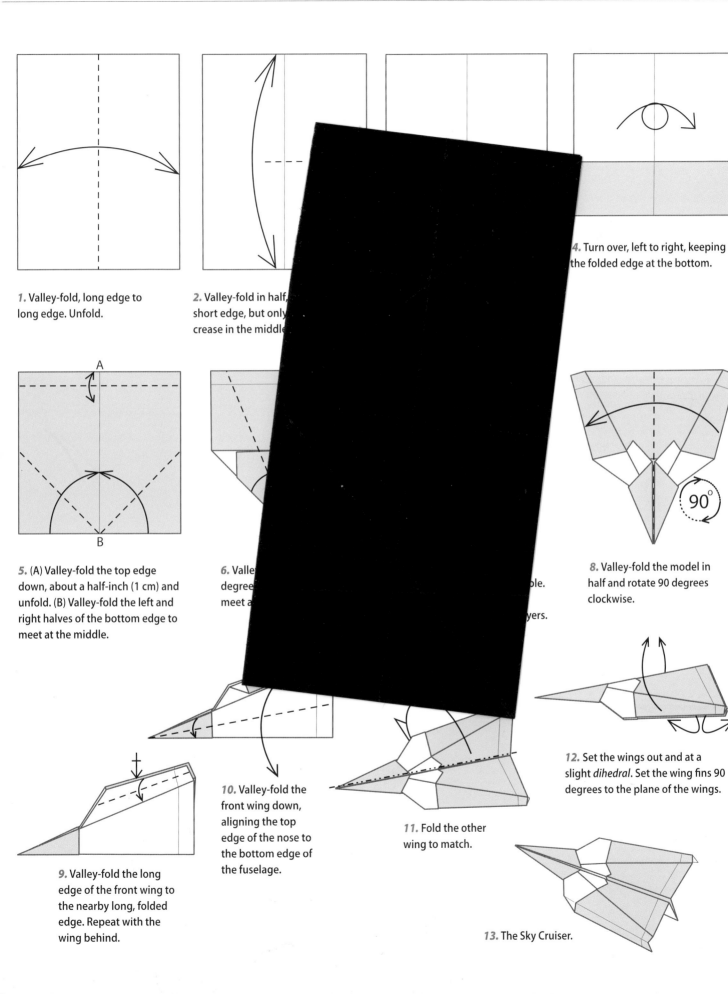

1. Valley-fold, long edge to long edge. Unfold.

2. Valley-fold in half, short edge, but only crease in the middle

4. Turn over, left to right, keeping the folded edge at the bottom.

5. (A) Valley-fold the top edge down, about a half-inch (1 cm) and unfold. (B) Valley-fold the left and right halves of the bottom edge to meet at the middle.

6. Valley
degree
meet a

8. Valley-fold the model in half and rotate 90 degrees clockwise.

9. Valley-fold the long edge of the front wing to the nearby long, folded edge. Repeat with the wing behind.

10. Valley-fold the front wing down, aligning the top edge of the nose to the bottom edge of the fuselage.

11. Fold the other wing to match.

12. Set the wings out and at a slight *dihedral*. Set the wing fins 90 degrees to the plane of the wings.

13. The Sky Cruiser.

AIRPLANE #13
THE TRANSFUSION

By Michael G. LaFosse

Here is one of my early attempts to improve the basic origami dart that I enjoyed flying in my youth. Step 3 shortens the plane and it adds weight to the nose. The extra layer makes a nose lock possible. Step 5 marks the paper for the angle of the leading edge of the wing and a convenient place to set up Step 12, which marks the paper in preparation for my squash fold elevon. These seemingly sympathetic geometries create a fine model, with good balance between forward weight and tail end resistance, and a very stable in-flight conformation. I love it when that happens!

Use 8 ½ by 11- inch US letter paper.

US
Letter

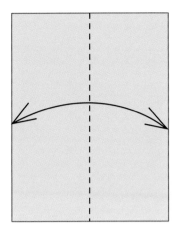

1. Valley-fold in half, long edge to long edge. Unfold.

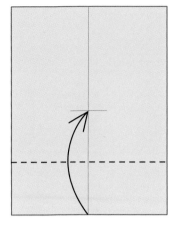

2. Valley-fold in half, bottom edge to top, but only crease a short distance across the middle. Unfold.

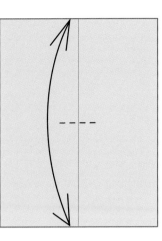

3. Valley-fold the bottom edge to the middle crease.

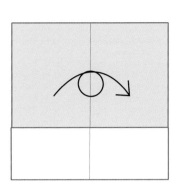

4. Turn over, left to right.

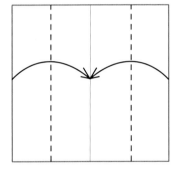

5. With the folded edge on the bottom, valley-fold the left and right edges to meet at the vertical center crease.

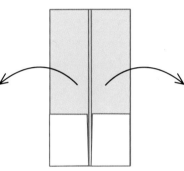

6. Unfold, returning the edges to the outside.

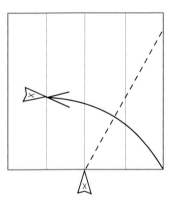

7. Valley-fold the bottom right corner to touch the far left crease, making the fold travel from the bottom of the center crease.

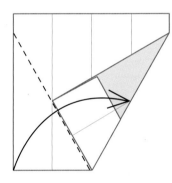

8. Valley-fold the bottom left corner and edge to meet the far right folded edge.

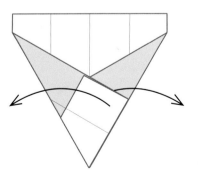

9. Unfold the last two folds.

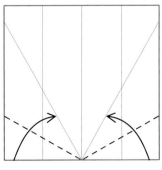

10. Valley-fold the left and right halves of the bottom edge to meet at the angled creases.

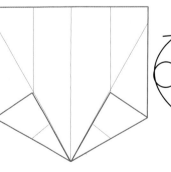

11. Turn the model over, top to bottom.

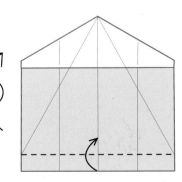

12. Valley-fold the bottom edge up, forming a cease at the level of the bottom ends of the angled creases.

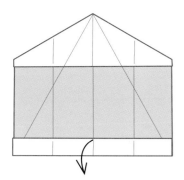

13. Unfold the last fold.

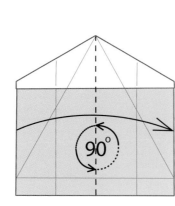

14. Valley-fold in half and rotate 90 degrees counterclockwise.

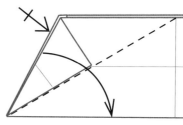

15. Using the existing creases, valley-fold the excess flaps of the wings down, forming the leading edge of the wings.

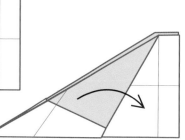

16. Spread the wings open.

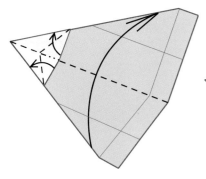

17. Valley-fold the creases for the nose lock by moving the free edge of the triangular top layer of the nose to the folded sides of the nose, once to the left and once to the right. Valley-fold the wings together while moving the free edge of the triangle layer forward.

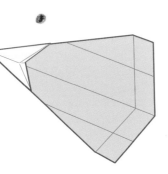

18. In progress: Forming the nose lock and bringing the wings together.

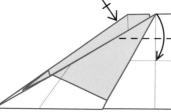

19. Valley-fold the short edges of the wings to the nearest crease, forming fins.

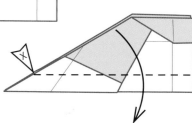

20. Beginning at the top of the nose lock, indicated with an "X." Fold the front wing down, parallel with the bottom of the fuselage.

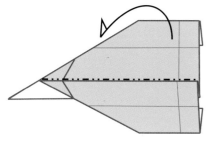

21. Mountain-fold the other wing to match.

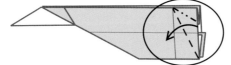

22. Make a valley crease, which spans from the top of the primary wing crease to the bottom corner of the wing. Squash-fold the elevons (details follow).

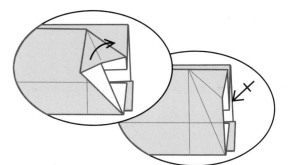

23. Move the foldable layer over the wing, forming a cone-shaped pocket. Flatten the pocket, aligning its center crease with the folded edge beneath it. Undo the squash fold, returning the back edge of the wing to its original place.

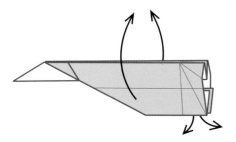

24. Set the wings straight out. Set tips at 90 degrees to the plane of the wings.

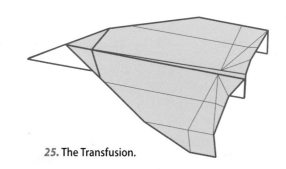

25. The Transfusion.

THE LOCK NOSE DARTS

By Michael G. LaFosse

The first paper planes that I learned to fold were the standard paper dart and a looping glider. They were quick and easy to make, and if you could finesse them: with a tweak here and a curl there, you could get them to fly very well. I must confess that as a young boy it seemed like magic when one of those simple darts performed at their best. However, most attempts were a bust, and (also like magic), the "secrets" seemed occult. One could always make these planes fly better by adding tape, staples, or paperclips; and perform better by tearing little tabs at the back of the wings to serve as elevons. As an origami enthusiast, these remedies were anathema to me; so, I sought to reach origami solutions to all of the problems I saw in these simple planes. Here's my list of grievances:

- The planes needed tape or staples to keep the nose closed and for added weight in the front;

- The planes needed fussy curling at the back of the wings, or torn tabs to serve as elevons;

- The planes had a sharply pointed nose, which was quickly bent out of shape when it hit the wall, or worse, dangerous if it should hit a bystander in the eye.

The nose lock that I devised takes care of issues number one and three, as it not only locks the nose but it blunts it and makes it fairly solid, too. Issue number two is addressed with a simple, but effective, single long elevon fold at the back of the model before the wings are formed. Locking the nose but not the fuselage preserves resiliency in the fuselage/wing zone, which I believe mitigates spiraling. This is now a true, one sheet, no appliances, no cut, no fuss, fold-and-fly dart. It is also an adaptable system: you can apply this origami technology to each of the three paper formats covered in this book. I hope that you will try them all.

AIRPLANE #14

LOCK NOSE DART: US LETTER PAPER—VARIATION A

Use an 8 ½ by 11-inch sheet of US letter paper, or a rectangle of similar proportions.

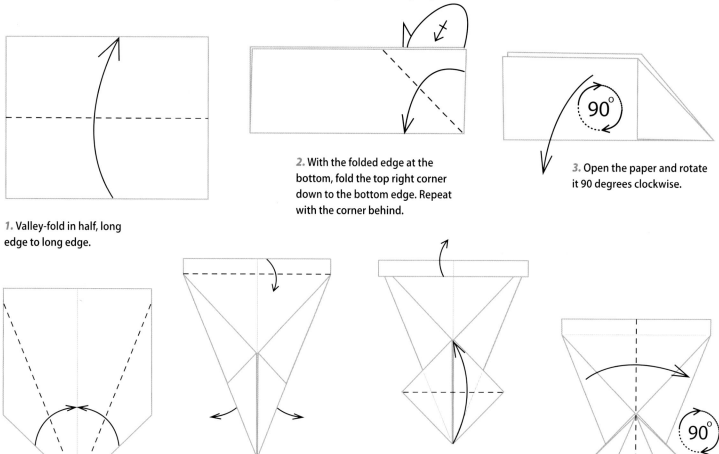

1. Valley-fold in half, long edge to long edge.

2. With the folded edge at the bottom, fold the top right corner down to the bottom edge. Repeat with the corner behind.

3. Open the paper and rotate it 90 degrees clockwise.

4. Valley-fold the bottom two folded edges to meet at the middle.

5. Move the hidden corners out from behind the bottom corner. Valley-fold the top edge down, making the crease span the distance between the two obtuse corners.

6. Return the top edge to its original position. Valley-fold the bottom square-diamond in half, bottom corner to top.

7. Valley-fold in half, left to right. Rotate 90 degrees clockwise.

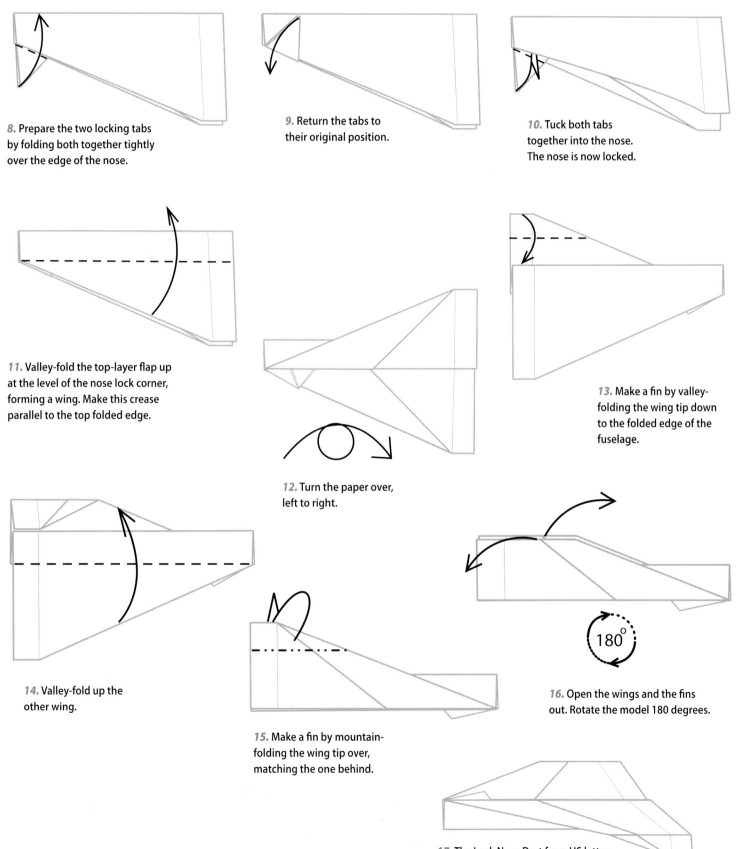

8. Prepare the two locking tabs by folding both together tightly over the edge of the nose.

9. Return the tabs to their original position.

10. Tuck both tabs together into the nose. The nose is now locked.

11. Valley-fold the top-layer flap up at the level of the nose lock corner, forming a wing. Make this crease parallel to the top folded edge.

12. Turn the paper over, left to right.

13. Make a fin by valley-folding the wing tip down to the folded edge of the fuselage.

14. Valley-fold up the other wing.

15. Make a fin by mountain-folding the wing tip over, matching the one behind.

16. Open the wings and the fins out. Rotate the model 180 degrees.

180°

17. The Lock Nose Dart from US letter paper, Variation A.

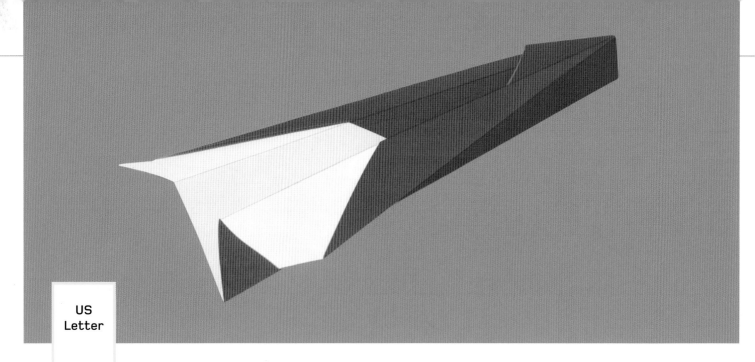

AIRPLANE #15

LOCK NOSE DART: US LETTER PAPER—variation B

Let's make another version of the Lock Nose Dart. Use an 8½ by 11-inch sheet of US letter paper, or a rectangle of similar proportions. Begin with the white side up if using trimmed origami paper.

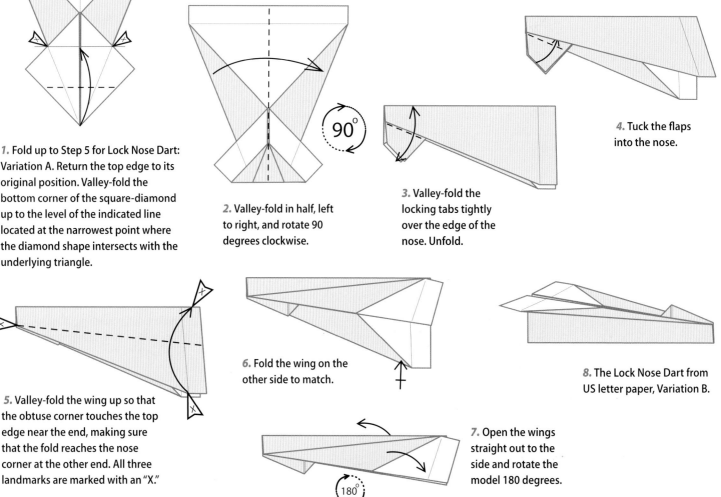

1. Fold up to Step 5 for Lock Nose Dart: Variation A. Return the top edge to its original position. Valley-fold the bottom corner of the square-diamond up to the level of the indicated line located at the narrowest point where the diamond shape intersects with the underlying triangle.

2. Valley-fold in half, left to right, and rotate 90 degrees clockwise.

3. Valley-fold the locking tabs tightly over the edge of the nose. Unfold.

4. Tuck the flaps into the nose.

5. Valley-fold the wing up so that the obtuse corner touches the top edge near the end, making sure that the fold reaches the nose corner at the other end. All three landmarks are marked with an "X."

6. Fold the wing on the other side to match.

7. Open the wings straight out to the side and rotate the model 180 degrees.

8. The Lock Nose Dart from US letter paper, Variation B.

AIRPLANE #16

LOCK NOSE DART:
square paper version

Let's adapt the Lock Nose Dart to square paper. Use a square from 6 to 10 inches. Begin with the white side up if using trimmed origami paper.

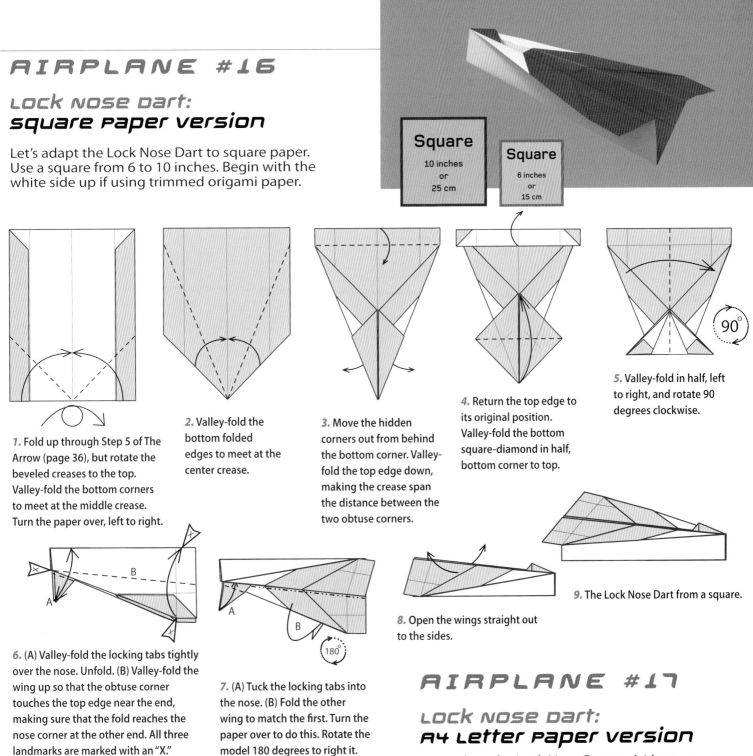

Square 10 inches or 25 cm

Square 6 inches or 15 cm

1. Fold up through Step 5 of The Arrow (page 36), but rotate the beveled creases to the top. Valley-fold the bottom corners to meet at the middle crease. Turn the paper over, left to right.

2. Valley-fold the bottom folded edges to meet at the center crease.

3. Move the hidden corners out from behind the bottom corner. Valley-fold the top edge down, making the crease span the distance between the two obtuse corners.

4. Return the top edge to its original position. Valley-fold the bottom square-diamond in half, bottom corner to top.

5. Valley-fold in half, left to right, and rotate 90 degrees clockwise.

6. (A) Valley-fold the locking tabs tightly over the nose. Unfold. (B) Valley-fold the wing up so that the obtuse corner touches the top edge near the end, making sure that the fold reaches the nose corner at the other end. All three landmarks are marked with an "X."

7. (A) Tuck the locking tabs into the nose. (B) Fold the other wing to match the first. Turn the paper over to do this. Rotate the model 180 degrees to right it.

8. Open the wings straight out to the sides.

9. The Lock Nose Dart from a square.

AIRPLANE #17

LOCK NOSE DART:
A4 letter paper version

Let's adapt the Lock Nose Dart to A4 letter paper.

1. Fold as for Lock Nose Dart, Variation A, with one exception: at Step 5, valley-fold the top edge of the paper to meet the obtuse corners of the wing paper. Continue folding as per Variation A.

2. The Lock Nose Dart from A4 letter paper.

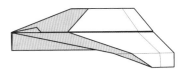

AIRPLANE #18
THE DOUBLE-FLAP
NOSE LOCK GLIDER

By Michael G. LaFosse

This simple-looking wing has an interesting setup: the fuselage tapers toward the back and is locked, keeping the wide back edges of the wings stable so that the large elevon flaps can do their job. Throw this wing gently.

You may use 8 ½ by 11-inch US letter paper or A4 letter paper for this airplane—both work equally well.

US Letter   **A4**

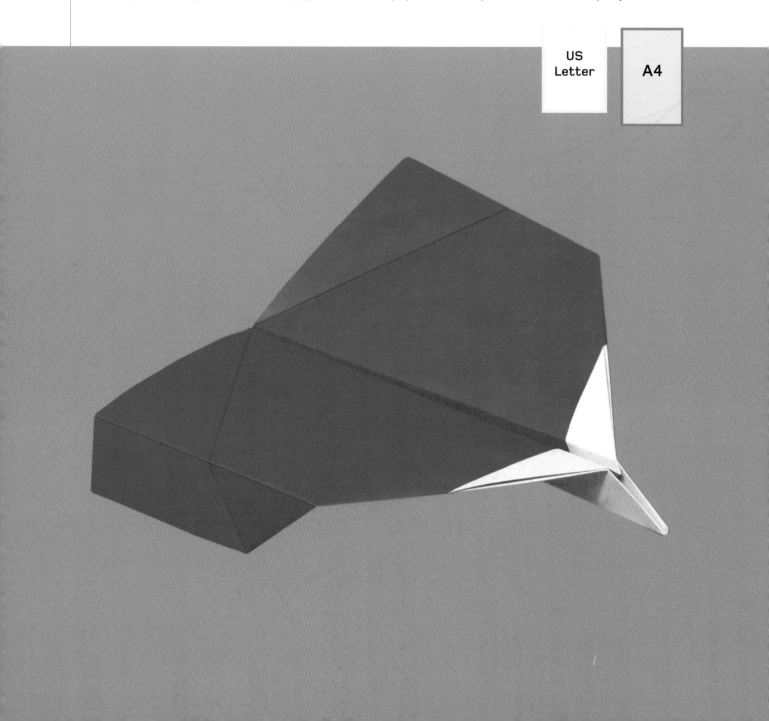

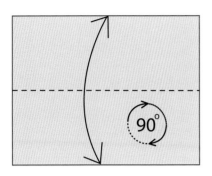

1. Valley-fold in half, long edge to long edge, and then unfold. Rotate the paper 90 degrees.

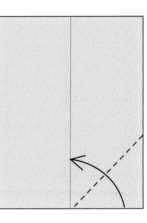

2. Valley-fold the right half of the bottom edge to the crease.

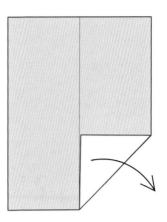

3. Unfold. This crease provides a landmark to set the proportions for the use of 8 ½ by 11-inch letter paper.

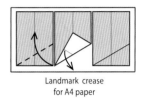

Landmark crease for A4 paper

3A. If using A4 paper: make a landmark crease as shown in the diagram and follow the folding sequence from there.

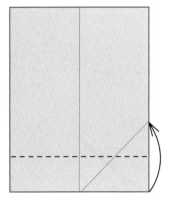

4. Valley-fold the bottom edge to the top of the landmark crease, forming a rectangular flap.

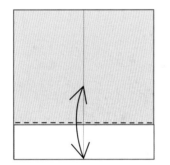

5. Valley-fold along the top edge of the rectangular flap. Unfold only this fold.

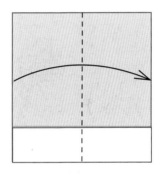

6. Valley-fold in half, long edge to long edge.

7. Valley-fold the folded edge to the crease, forming a triangular flap.

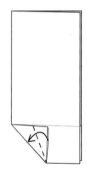

8. Valley-fold the right edge of the triangle flap to the long edge of the flap.

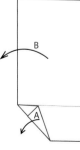

9. (A) Unfold the triangle flap. (B) Open the paper.

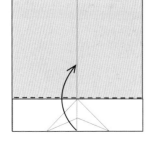

10. Use the existing crease to fold the bottom flap up.

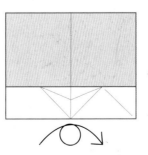

11. Turn over, left to right.

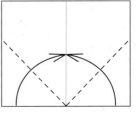

12. The folded edge should be at the bottom. Valley-fold the left and right halves of the bottom edge to meet at the middle.

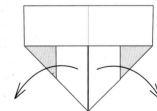

13. Unfold.

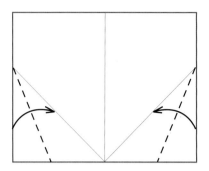

14. Valley-fold the left and right side edges to the 45 degree angled creases.

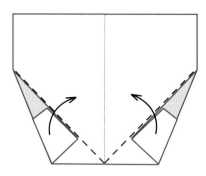

15. Use the existing creases to valley-fold the triangle flaps in.

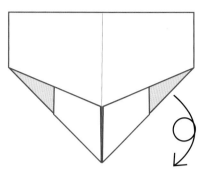

16. Turn over, top to bottom.

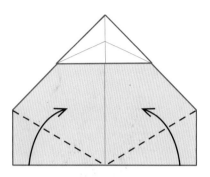

17. Valley-fold the left and right halves of the bottom edge up. The crease should span from the middle of the bottom to the obtuse corners of the wings.

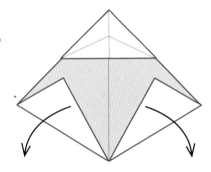

18. Unfold the indicated flaps.

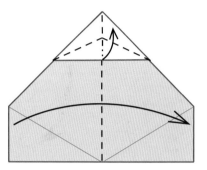

19. Lift up the free edge of the triangular paper at the top. Use the existing creases, valley-fold the model in half and move the triangle's free edge into the nose, forming the nose lock.

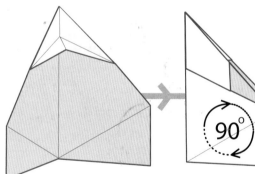

20. Nose lock in progress. Rotate the model 90 degrees clockwise.

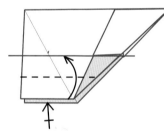

21. Make stabilizers by valley-folding the ends of the wings up to the level indicated by the horizontal red line. This line is level with the layered edge visible on the leading edge of the wings.

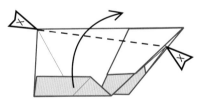

22. Valley-fold the first wing. The crease should span the square corner at the back of the model and the layered, folded corner inside the nose. This will accomplish the nose lock.

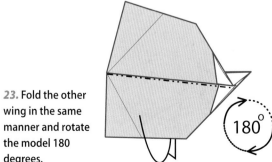

23. Fold the other wing in the same manner and rotate the model 180 degrees.

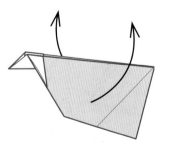

24. Open the wings out to each side and set the stabilizer flaps perpendicular to the wings. The wings can be level, or they can have a slight *dihedral* ("Y" shape).

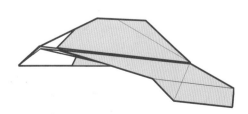

25. The Double-Flap Nose Lock Glider.

AIRPLANE #19
THE PELICAN

By Michael G. LaFosse

The nose of this model is a large triangular bucket, much like the bill of a pelican. Transforming this portion of the model is an interesting and satisfying origami process. It is one of those maneuvers quite difficult to explain in a diagram, but it is easy to understand when you see the video. You may notice that when a breeze buffets this plane from either side, one wing may lift, taking the brunt of it, preventing the plane from flipping over or spiraling out of control. It is the open fuselage that makes this model so resilient in flight. This gentle glider works best when dropped from a height, or launched softly.

Use a sheet of 8 ½ by 11-inch US letter paper, or smaller size of the same proportions.

US
Letter

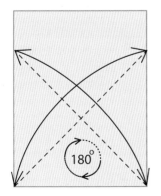

1. Valley-fold the short bottom edge to meet one of the long edges. Unfold. Valley-fold the bottom edge to the other long edge. Unfold. Rotate the paper 180 degrees.

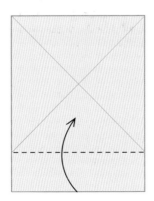

2. Valley-fold the bottom edge up to the ends of the crossing creases.

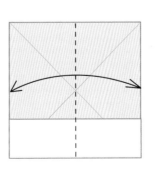

3. Valley-fold in half, long edge to long edge. Unfold.

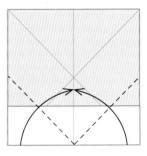

4. Valley-fold the left and right halves of the bottom edge to meet at the middle.

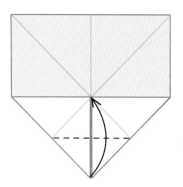

5. Valley-fold the bottom corner up to meet the intersection of creases and corners.

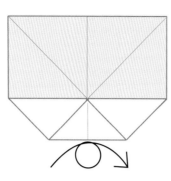

6. Turn over, left to right.

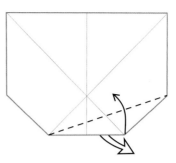

7. Valley-fold the bottom right corner up. The crease should span the bottom left and the right side obtuse corners. Allow the triangular flap to come out from under the model.

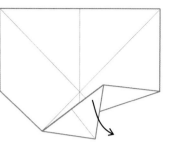

8. Return the corner and flap to their original place.

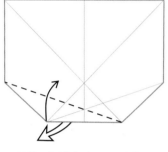

9. Valley-fold the bottom left corner up. The crease should span the bottom right and the left side obtuse corners. Allow the triangular flap to come out from under the model.

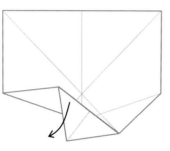

10. Return the corner and flap to their original place.

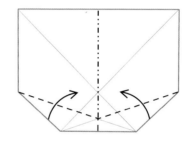

11. Use existing creases to form the leading edges of the wings and the glider's nose. Fold the wing's leading edges simultaneously, while mountain-folding the model in half.

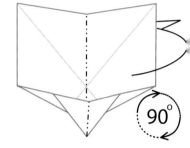

12. Folding in progress. Bring the wings together and rotate the model 90 degrees clockwise.

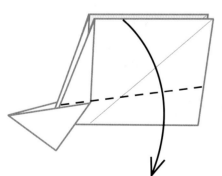

13. Valley-fold the front wing down. Use the top edge of the nose structure to guide the angle.

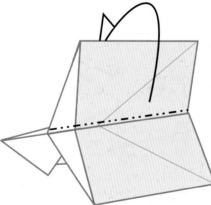

14. Fold the other wing to match.

15. (A) Valley-fold the back edge of the wing to the crease. Unfold. Repeat on the other wing. (B) Set the wings straight out to each side.

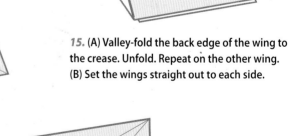

16. The Pelican.

AIRPLANE #20
THE NIFTY FIFTY

By Michael G. LaFosse

Here is an early model of mine, developed in 1978, with deliberate styling inspired by the older cars sporting fins that I remember cruising the streets of my youth! These cars seemed so futuristic back then; TV "westerns" were waning in popularity, slowly being replaced with shows and movies about rocket ships and space adventures. The style was everywhere in the 1950s. As a kid, one of my favorite TV shows was *Fireball XL-5*, and those of you familiar with this show may recognize that influence in the long vertical tail and the wings' tip fins.

Use 8½ by 11-inch US letter paper or A4 letter paper.

The Nifty Fifty is the first model for which I developed the nose lock that I would later use in my Flying Fox and Nose Lock series of improved classic dart designs.

US
Letter

A4

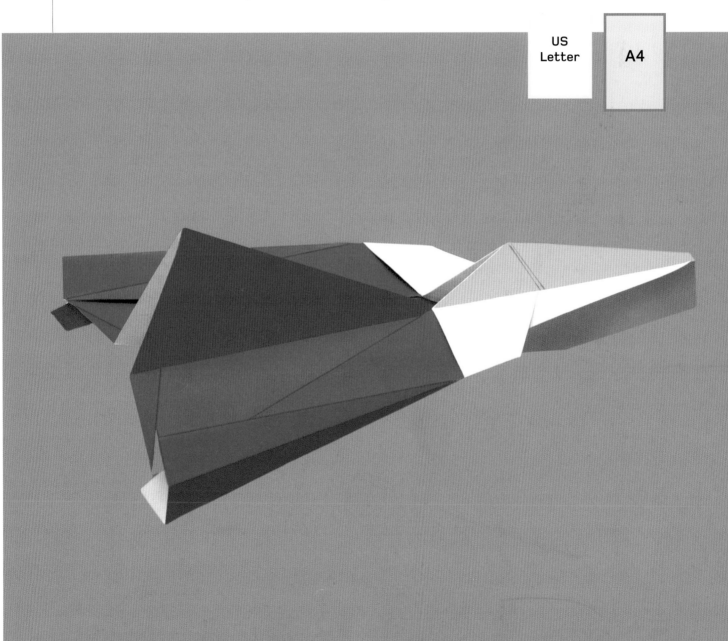

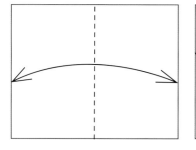

1. Valley-fold in half, short edge to short edge. Unfold.

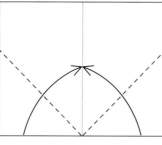

2. Valley-fold the left and right halves of the bottom edge to meet at the middle.

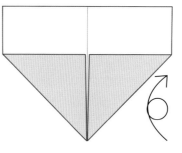

3. Turn over, top to bottom.

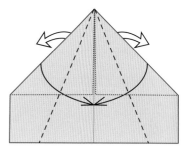

4. Valley-fold the 45-degree angle edges to meet at the middle. Allow the hidden triangular flaps to move to the front.

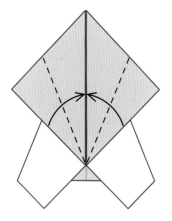

5. Valley-fold the bottom edges of the square diamond area to meet at the middle.

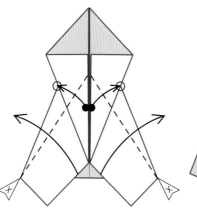

6. Valley-fold the wings out. Notice the landmarks for proper alignment.

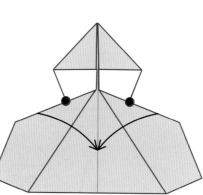

7. Return the wings to the middle.

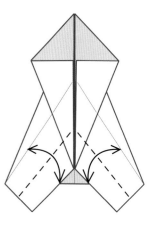

8. Valley-fold the inside back edges of the wings to meet the creases formed in Step 6. Unfold.

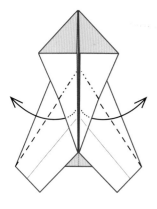

9. Use the creases formed in Step 6 to inside-reverse-fold the wings out.

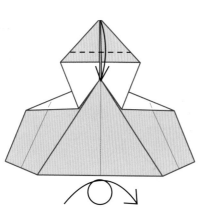

10. Valley-fold the nose corner to the V-notch. Turn over, left to right.

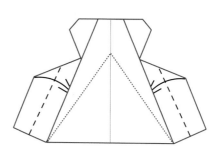

11. Use the crease formed in Step 8 to tuck the outer edges of the wings behind the folded layers.

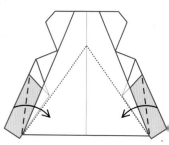

12. Valley-fold the outer corners of the wings to form the fins.

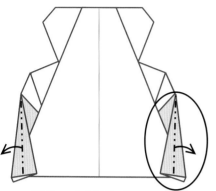

13. Squash-fold the fins.

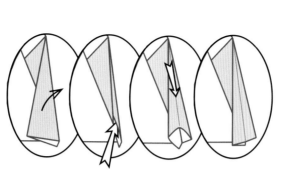

14. Squash-folding details.

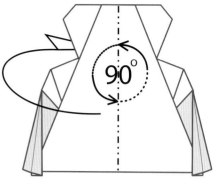

15. Mountain-fold in half, wing to wing. Rotate 90 degrees counterclockwise.

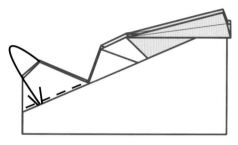

16. Tuck the two paper nose tabs into one side of the nose, forming a nose lock.

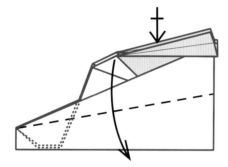

17. Fold both wings down. The top of the nose lock at the front of the model and the back of the nose lock, inside the model, will set the proper wing angle for you.

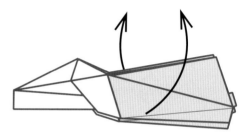

18. Return the wings straight up.

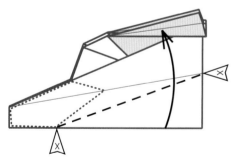

19. Valley-fold the back corner of the fuselage up. The fold should span from the back end of the wing-fold crease to the place in the front where the paper becomes thick.

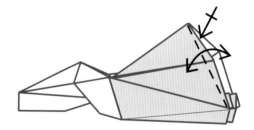

20. Return the corner to the bottom. Fold the wings down on each side and inside-reverse fold the tail up. (See *Flying Fox* step 28 on page 46.)

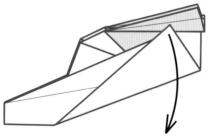

21. Form elevon flaps by valley-folding the back edges of the wings and the vertical tail. Unfold. These elevons are narrow but they are very effective. Do not omit this step.

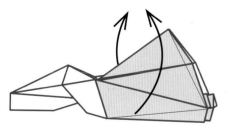

22. Set the wings straight out to the sides.

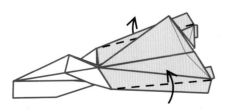

23. Adjust the wing fins so that they are perpendicular to the wings.

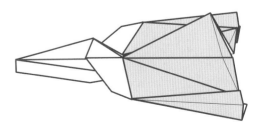

24. The Nifty Fifty.

AIRPLANE #21
THE HOUSE FLY

By Michael G. LaFosse

The general top-view outline of this plane—with its side-by-side rectangular front flaps, like a geometric abstract of a fly's eyes—always makes me think of this little pest. Well, what's in a name?

This model is an excellent glider. In 1995 I applied the fuselage lock that I had just developed, making it a solid little paper plane. You can throw this one with full force. You can also experiment with different fin designs and even add some elevons to make it climb high or loop.

Use letter paper, either 8½ by 11-inch or A4. Both will work well.

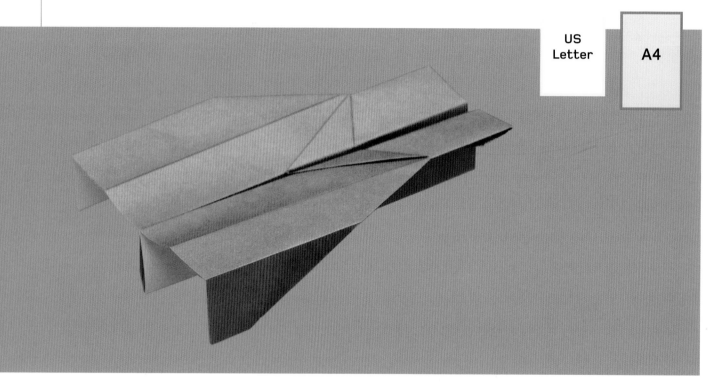

US
Letter

A4

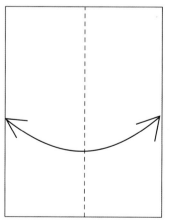

1. Valley-fold in half, long edge to long edge. Unfold.

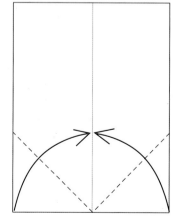

2. Valley-fold the left and right halves of the bottom edge to meet at the crease.

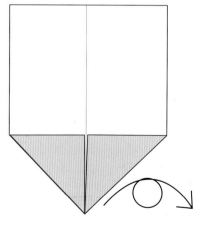

3. Turn over, left to right.

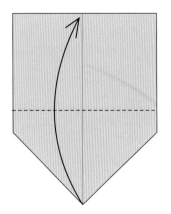

4. Fold the bottom corner up to meet the middle of the top edge.

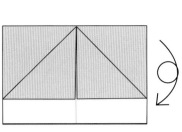

5. Turn over, top to bottom.

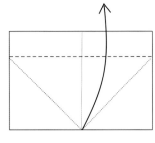

6. The folded edge should be at the top. Valley-fold the bottom edge up so that the crease is level with the top edges of the triangle flaps underneath. X-ray lines are displayed in the drawing for reference.

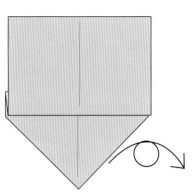

7. Your paper should look like this. Turn over, left to right.

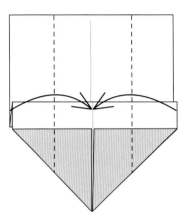

8. Valley-fold the left and right edges to meet at the middle.

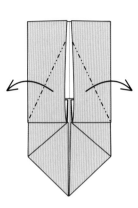

9. Open each of the top layers of the upper area and squash-fold outward, forming the wings. The mountain crease will form upon final flattening.

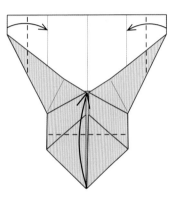

10. Valley-fold the bottom corner up to meet the intersection paper layers at the center crease, forming a blunt nose. Valley-fold the ends of each wing to meet at the nearest crease, forming the stabilizers.

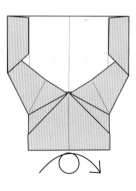

11. Your paper should look like this. Turn over, left to right.

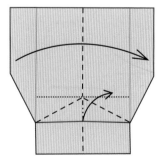

12. Form the fuselage lock by first lifting up the free edge of paper above the nose edge. Install two valley creases that span from the middle of the top limit—shown by the X-ray line—to the bottom left and right limits of the paper's free edge. Valley-fold the model in half.

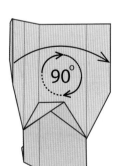

13. Fuselage lock and folding in half in progress. Close the model flat and rotate 90 degrees clockwise.

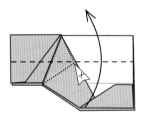

14. Valley-fold the first wing up. Note the limiting point, marked with an "X," which represents the fuselage lock fold inside. The wings are to be folded at this level.

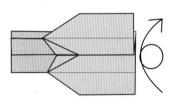

15. Your model will look like this. Turn over, top to bottom.

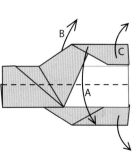

16. (A) Valley-fold the other wing to match the first. (B) Set the wings to be straight out to each side. (C) Set the stabilizers to be perpendicular to the wings.

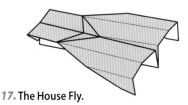

17. The House Fly.

AIRPLANE #22
THE CANARD CRUISER

By Michael G. LaFosse

This little gem has gone through many a makeover. My earliest notes go back to 1993, and I was excited by its promise. By 1996, I had tweaked the design to the point that I considered it good enough to publish, and I decided to share it in our video, *Aerogami*. I improved this design once again when we revisited *Aerogami* to add new material and menus on DVD, to focus on models for the non-square, rectangular format. This book gave me an opportunity to give the Canard Cruiser another look, and this makeover makes this design the best yet. We left the keel down, instead of inside-reverse-folding it up for a tail, this simple modification made the plane stable enough to forgo adding the wing flaps. If you are a longtime fan of our planes, you will appreciate its improved performance from the single, long, elevon that I added. This excellent glider looks great in flight, but it is an advanced model, so hone your skills before challenging yourself.

Use 8½ by 11-inch US letter or A4 letter paper.

US
Letter

A4

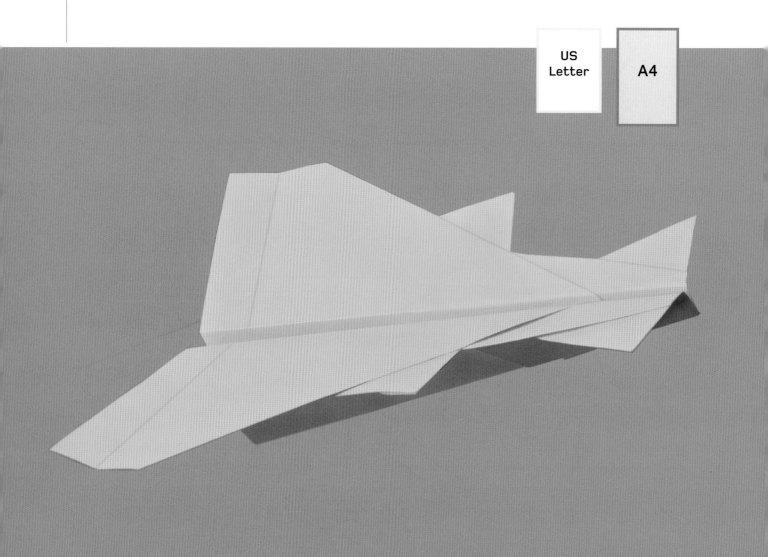

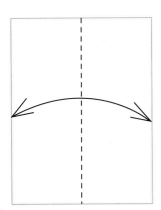

1. Valley-fold, long edge to long edge. Unfold.

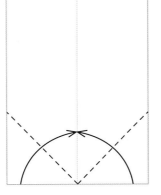

2. Valley-fold the left and right halves of the bottom edge to meet at the crease.

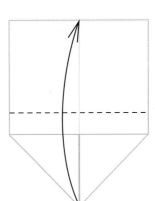

3. Fold the bottom corner up to meet the middle of the top edge.

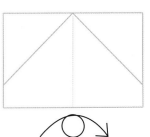

4. Turn over, left to right.

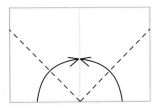

5. The folded edge should be at the bottom.

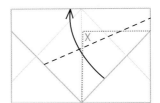

6. (A) Return the triangle flaps to the bottom. (B) Turn over, top to bottom.

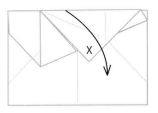

7. Valley-fold the 45-degree angle edge from the right side of the front flap up to meet the top edge. Allow the hidden triangle flap to come out from behind.

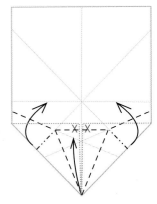

8. Return the flap to the original position.

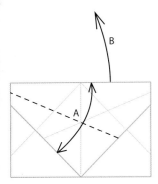

9. (A) Repeat Steps 7 and 8 on the left side. (B) Unfold the back flap up.

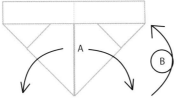

10. Valley-fold the bottom 45-degree angle edges to meet at the middle, but crease only to the level of the horizontal center crease.

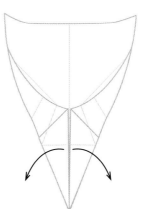

11. Bring the edges back down.

12. Use the existing creases to make the nose corner stand up, perpendicular to the rest of the paper. Move the left and right side creases simultaneously to do this. Allow the hidden triangle flaps, marked with "X"s, to come out from behind.

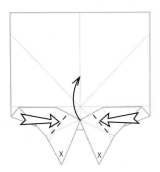

13. Push in the side panels of the standing nose corner and flatten the shape onto the paper above. Look ahead at the diagram for Step 14 for the shape.

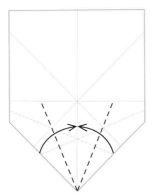

14. Mountain-fold the structure behind the top half of the sheet.

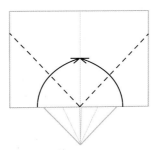

15. Valley-fold the left and right edges of the rectangular area to meet at the middle.

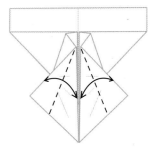

16. Your paper should look like this. Valley-fold and unfold the top edges of the square diamond area.

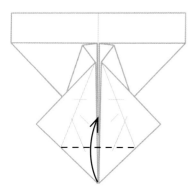

17. Valley-fold the bottom corner up. The fold should span between the bottom ends of the creases formed in Step 16.

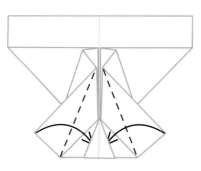

18. Use the existing creases to tuck the left and right corners into the triangle pockets in the nose.

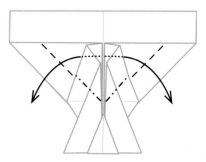

19. Inside-reverse-fold the layered corners out, perpendicular to the vertical centerline, forming the wings.

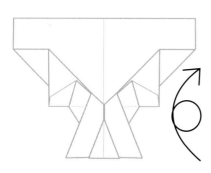

20. Turn the model over, top to bottom.

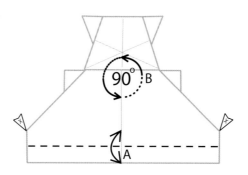

21. (A) Valley-fold the bottom edge up, square corners meeting with the obtuse corners, above. Unfold. (B) Rotate the model 90 degrees counter clockwise.

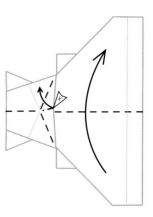

22. Form the fuselage lock by lifting up the free edge of paper near the middle of the model. Valley-fold along the crossing creases to describe a triangle, and valley-fold the model in half, matching wing to wing.

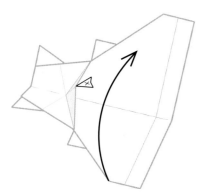

23. Folding in progress. The edge with the "X" mark will move up and forward as the model is flattened.

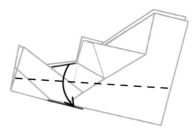

24. Valley-fold the front wing down, matching the two edges highlighted in red.

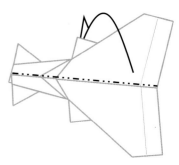

25. Fold the other wing to match.

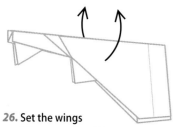

26. Set the wings straight out to the sides.

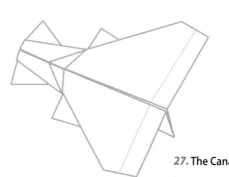

27. The Canard Cruiser.

AIRPLANE #23
THE FUSELAGE-LOCK SWEET DART

By Michael G. LaFosse

Outside of square paper, my favorite format from which to design new origami planes is our standard 8 ½ by 11-inch US letter paper. The Sky Cruiser (page 54) design convinced me that US letter paper produced better flying airplanes when it was shortened, by folding one edge over at the nose. This folded edge not only improved the proportions of the planes, but it also added needed weight to the front. I was also familiar with A4 paper and its rectangular proportions of 1: √2, through Eiji Nakamur's marvelous book *Flying Origami, Origami From Pure Fun to True Science*, (Japan Publications, 1972). I began to experiment with this format, too, but I found the proportions too long and narrow for the strategies that I was pursuing. However, trying to sufficiently shorten the A4 sheets did point to a breakthrough for me: I put a mountain/valley crimp in the middle of the sheet to take up some slack. This middle overlap provided movable layers to develop wings, and eventually, my fuselage lock. I applied the technique to US letter paper. This dart is the first in the series of fuselage locked models that I developed, beginning in 1990.

Use a sheet of 8 ½ by 11-inch US letter paper.

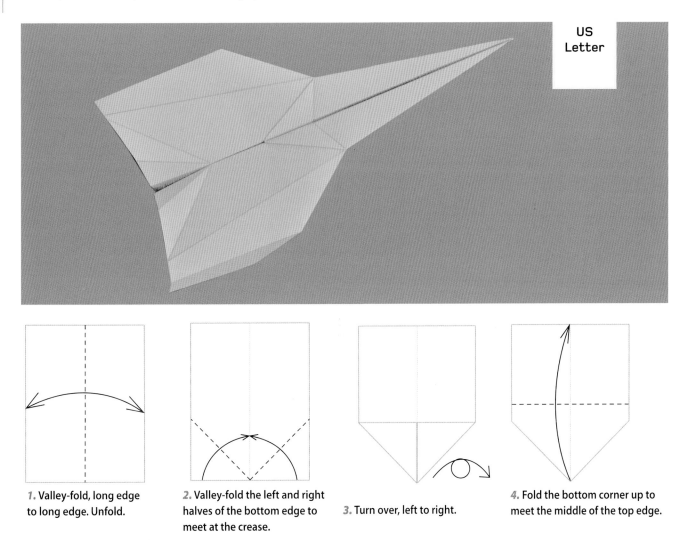

US Letter

1. Valley-fold, long edge to long edge. Unfold.

2. Valley-fold the left and right halves of the bottom edge to meet at the crease.

3. Turn over, left to right.

4. Fold the bottom corner up to meet the middle of the top edge.

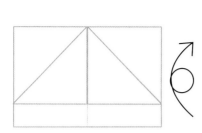

5. Turn over, bottom to top.

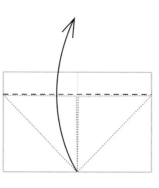

6. The folded edge should be at the top. Valley-fold the bottom edge up so that the crease is level with the top edges of the triangle flaps underneath. X-ray lines are displayed in the drawing for reference.

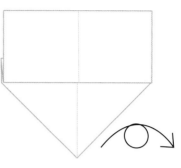

7. Your paper should look like this. Turn over, left to right.

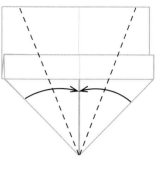

8. Valley-fold to make the 45-degree angled bottom edges meet at the middle.

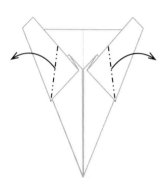

9. Squash-fold the top layers of the upper area outward, forming the wings.

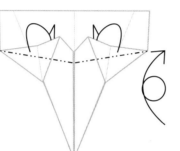

10. Mountain-fold the free edges of the undersides of the wings to make them trim. Turn over, top to bottom.

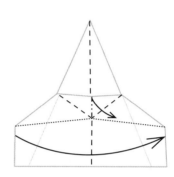

11. Form the fuselage lock by first lifting the free edge of paper at the level just below the nose. Install two valley creases that span from the middle of the bottom limit—shown by the X-ray line—to the top left and right limits of the paper's free edge. Valley-fold the model in half.

12. This shows the fuselage lock, and folding in half, both in progress. Close the model flat and rotate 90 degrees counterclockwise.

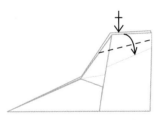

13. Valley-fold the top edge of the wing to match the crease, below, forming a fin. Repeat with the other wing.

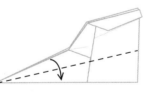

14. Valley-fold the first wing down, aligning the nose-edge to the bottom edge of the fuselage. The fold will continue through the fuselage lock and set the angle for the wing.

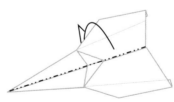

15. Fold the other wing to match.

16. Folding the elevons: Valley-fold the back edge of a wing to meet the long crease on the wing, forming a layered triangle flap.

17. Open the two layers of the triangle flap and squash-fold. Undo the squash-fold and return the flap to the back edge of the wing. These valley and mountain creases make attractive control surfaces, and they are very effective. They can be easily adjusted, too.

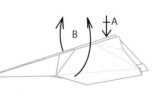

18. (A) Repeat the elevon folds on the other wing. (B) Set both wings out straight and level and set the fins 90 degrees from the plane of the wing.

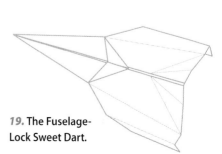

19. The Fuselage-Lock Sweet Dart.

AIRPLANE #24
THE SAFE-T-DART

By Michael G. LaFosse

The Fuselage-Lock Sweet Dart was an exciting development and I loved to make and fly them. But I was concerned about safety issues with pointed-nose planes. Blunt-nosed planes are less dangerous—but they can still hurt if you get hit. I have long appreciated that the extra folded layers concentrate more weight in the nose, making a model that can be thrown further. I blunted the nose of the Fuselage-Lock Sweet Dart at Step 8 and now we have a dart that can fly farther while posing less of a danger.

For more fun, make a second Safe-T-Dart from a smaller sheet, say 5 ½ by 7 inches, and load it into the slot at the nose of the full-size model. Launch them as one and they will separate in flight, each gliding their own way.

Use 8 ½ by 11-inch US letter paper.

US
Letter

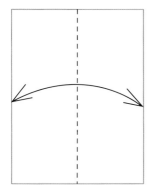

1. Valley-fold, long edge to long edge. Unfold.

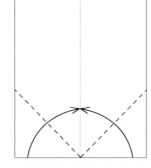

2. Valley-fold the left and right halves of the bottom edge to meet at the crease.

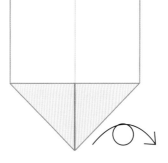

3. Turn over, left to right.

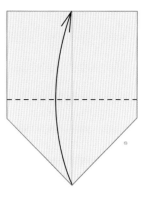

4. Fold the bottom corner up to meet the middle of the top edge.

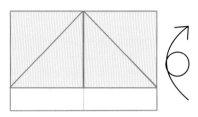

5. Turn over, bottom to top.

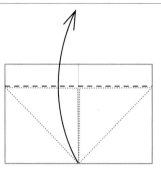

6. The folded edge should be at the top. Valley-fold the bottom edge up so that the crease is level with the top edges of the triangular flaps underneath. X-ray lines are displayed in the drawing for reference.

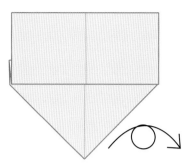

7. Your paper should look like this. Turn over, left to right.

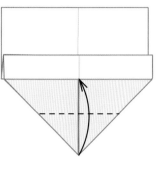

8. Valley-fold the bottom corner to the top of the split where the two square corners meet.

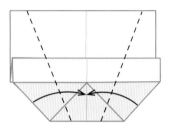

9. Valley-fold to make the 45-degree angled side edges meet at the middle.

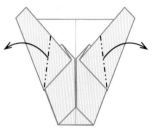

10. Squash-fold the top layers of the upper area outward, forming the wings.

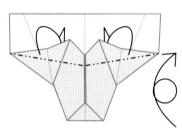

11. Mountain-fold the free edges of the undersides of the wings to make them trim. Turn over, top to bottom.

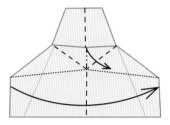

12. Form the fuselage lock by first lifting the free edge of paper at the level just below the nose. Install two valley creases that span from the middle of the bottom limit—shown by the X-ray line—to the top left and right limits of the paper's free edge. Valley-fold the model in half.

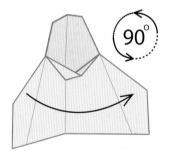

13. This diagram shows the fuselage lock, and the folding in half, both in progress. Close the model flat and rotate 90 degrees counterclockwise.

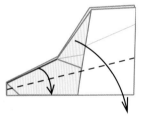

14. Valley-fold the first wing down, aligning the nose-edge—highlighted in red line—to the bottom edge of the fuselage. The wing fold will continue through the fuselage lock and set the angle for this fold.

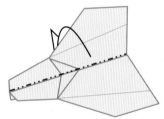

15. Fold the other wing to match.

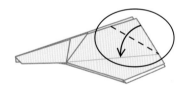

16. Folding the elevons: Valley-fold the back edge of a wing to meet the long crease on the wing, forming a layered triangular flap.

17. Open the two layers of the triangular flap and squash-fold. Undo the squash-fold and return the flap to the back edge of the wing. These valley and mountain creases make attractive control surfaces. They are remarkably effective and are easily adjusted.

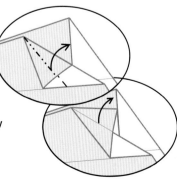

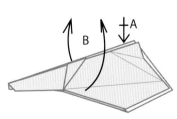

18. (A) Repeat the elevon folds on the other wing. (B) Set both wings out straight and level. You can also add wing fins if you wish. See Step 13 of the Fuselage-Lock Sweet Dart.

19. The Safe-T-Dart

AIRPLANE #25
THE STDC
(SAFE-T-DART WITH CANARD)

By Michael G. LaFosse

In the early 1990s I was developing a folding system for a family of planes that would have a lot of variability in both the nose and the wing configurations. Some of these darts had pointed noses, but the ones that performed the best were blunt. Because the blunt-nosed versions present less of a risk of injury, I named the collection "Safe-T-Dart." In 1995 I developed a fuselage lock for my designs. It took advantage of the overlapping layers near the middle of the fuselage (see Steps 12–15). It is quite effective, and attractive, too. We first published this new bit of origami paper airplane technology in the 1996 release of our video, *Aerogami*.

Of the dozens of Safe-T-Dart designs that I have developed, this one is my favorite. The canards are a nice touch, both aesthetically and functionally, and the elevon system that I developed, and also refer to as "wing faceting," gives the total design an integrated, geometric, functional form that is both stylish and complimentary. It is a pleasure to fold, too!

Use 8 ½ by 11-inch US letter paper.

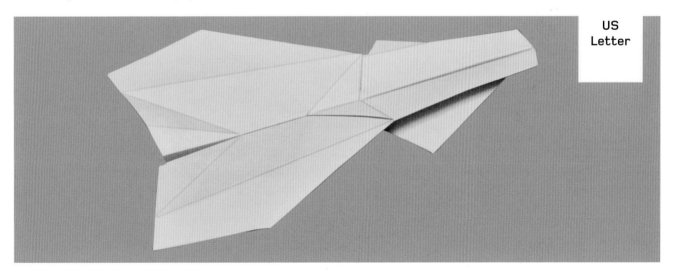

US Letter

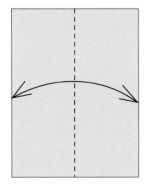

1. Valley-fold, long edge to long edge. Unfold.

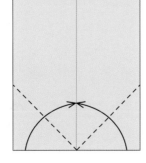

2. Valley-fold the left and right halves of the bottom edge to meet at the crease.

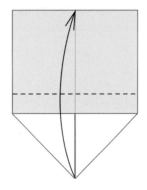

3. Fold the bottom corner up to meet the middle of the top edge.

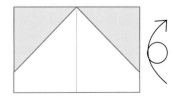

4. Turn over, top to bottom.

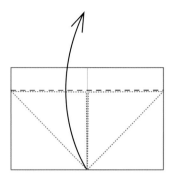

5. The folded edge should be at the top. Valley-fold the bottom edge up so that the crease is level with the top edges of the triangle flaps underneath. X-ray lines are displayed in the drawing for reference.

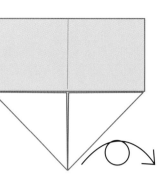

6. Your paper should look like this. Turn over, left to right.

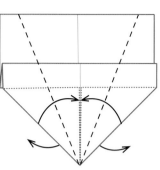

7. Valley-fold to make the 45-degree angled bottom edges meet at the middle. Allow the triangle flaps to move with the paper, from the back to the front.

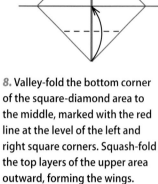

8. Valley-fold the bottom corner of the square-diamond area to the middle, marked with the red line at the level of the left and right square corners. Squash-fold the top layers of the upper area outward, forming the wings.

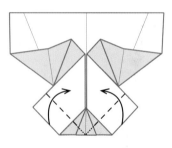

9. Shape the canard by valley-folding the indicated edges inward. Note that the creases must meet at the middle of the bottom, inside the layers of the nose.

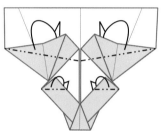

10. Mountain-fold the free edges of the undersides of the wings to make them trim. Mountain-fold the square corner flaps of the canard paper, making them trim.

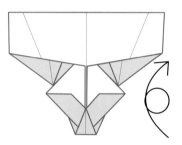

11. Your paper should look like this. Turn over, top to bottom.

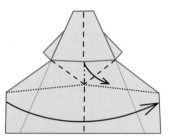

12. Form the fuselage lock by first lifting the free edge of paper at the level just below the canards. Install two valley creases that span from the middle of the bottom limit—shown by the X-ray line—to the top left and right limits of the paper's free edge. Valley-fold the model in half.

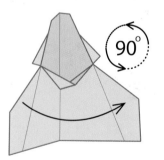

13. This diagram shows the fuselage lock, and the folding in half, both in progress. Close the model flat and rotate 90 degrees counterclockwise.

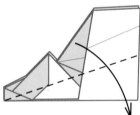

14. Valley-fold the first wing down. The crease should run from the bottom corner of the nose and through the top corner of the folded fuselage lock, which is between the wings.

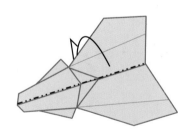

15. Fold the other wing to match.

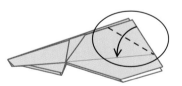

16. Folding the elevons: Valley-fold the back edge of a wing to meet the long crease on the wing, forming a layered triangle flap.

17. Open the two layers of the triangle flap and squash-fold. Undo the squash-fold and return the flap to the back edge of the wing. These valley and mountain creases make attractive control surfaces, and they are very effective. They can be easily adjusted, too.

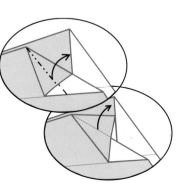

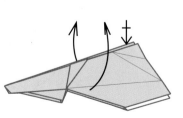

18. Repeat the elevon folds on the other wing and set both wings out straight and level.

19. The STDC (Safe-T-Dart with Canard).

AIRPLANE #26
THE WHISKER JET

By Michael G. LaFosse

I arrived at this model after a couple years of folding new designs from my Fuselage Lock Dart series; again returning to the square format—"home" for many of us origami practitioners. We first convert the square to a rectangle with the approximate proportions of US letter paper by folding in $1/8^{th}$ of the square from each of two opposite edges. The extra layers are always a bonus. I was pleased when they cooperated to neatly form these smart-looking canard wings, which proved so effective that elevons are not needed for this version of the Fuselage Lock series.

Use paper at least 8 inches, square. Larger origami paper (10 inches) is also excellent for this model.

Square

10 inches
or
25 cm

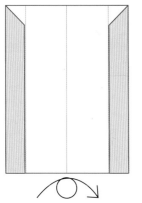

1. Fold up through Step 5 of the Arrow (page 35) and rotate your paper so that the beveled folds appear at the top of the paper, as illustrated here. Turn the paper over, left to right.

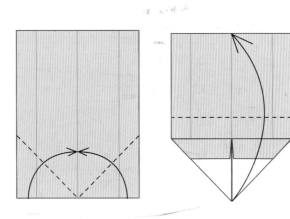

2. Valley-fold the left and right halves of the bottom edge to meet at the crease.

3. Fold the bottom corner up to meet the middle of the top edge.

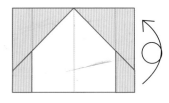

4. Turn over, bottom to top.

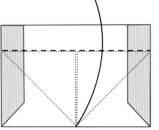

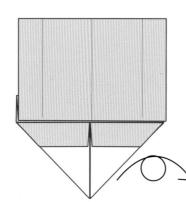

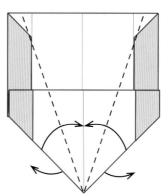

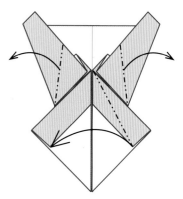

5. The folded edge should be at the top. Valley-fold the bottom edge up so that the crease is level with the top edges of the triangle flaps underneath. X-ray lines are displayed in the drawing for reference.

6. Your paper should look like this. Turn over, left to right.

7. Valley-fold to make the 45-degree angled bottom edges meet at the middle. Allow the triangular flaps to move to the front.

8. Squash-fold the top layers of the upper area outward, forming the wings. Squash-fold the right side flap in the square-diamond area of the nose.

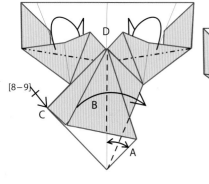

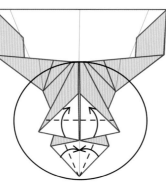

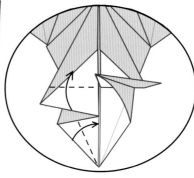

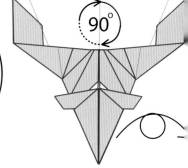

9. (A) Valley-fold the indicated edge to the center crease. Unfold. (B) Move the nose flap to the right. (C) Repeat Steps 8 and 9 on the left nose flap. (D) Mountain-fold the free edges of the undersides of the wings to make them trim.

10. Forming the canards. Detail follows.

11. Form each canard, one at a time. Use the existing crease in the nose corner to valley-fold the side edge in toward the center, then lift the free edge of the canard and valley-fold it over, forming a small wing. Repeat with other side.

12. Rotate the model 90 degrees clockwise and turn over to the other side.

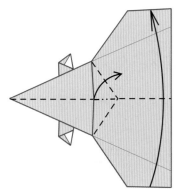

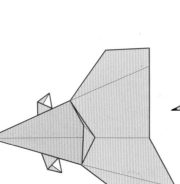

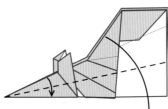

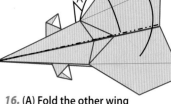

13. Form the fuselage lock by lifting the free edge of paper at the center, while valley-folding the model in half.

14. This diagram shows the fuselage lock, and the folding in half, both in progress.

15. Valley-fold the first wing down, aligning the nose-edge to the bottom edge of the fuselage. The wing fold will continue through the fuselage lock and set the angle for this fold.

16. (A) Fold the other wing to match. (B) Set the wings straight out to the sides.

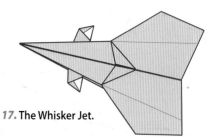

17. The Whisker Jet.

AIRPLANE #27
THE DUCK BILL DOLLAR CANARD

By Michael G. LaFosse

Designing paper airplanes has been a favorite pastime for me ever since I was a young boy. Folding scraps of paper, while waiting for one thing or another, or during long bus or car trips, is relaxing and absorbing. I designed this little plane during a long car ride between Williamstown and Fitchburg, Massachusetts, sometime in 1977. The dollar was unfolded and used to buy gasoline along the way, but I never forgot how to fold the simple design. It also works well when folded from ordinary paper, enlarged and cut to the same proportions as a US dollar bill. One of the lessons in our *Trash Origami* book and DVD set is that soup can labels have similar proportions to a dollar bill, and you can make great dollar bill origami projects by folding soup labels instead!

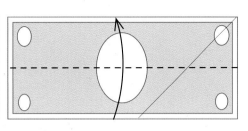

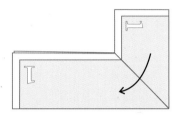

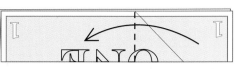

3. Valley-fold a portion of the right side over to the left. Use the top end of the crease line from Step 1 as a guide.

1. Begin with either side of the bill facing up. Valley-fold the short, right side up to the top edge. Unfold.

2. Valley-fold the bottom edge up to the top edge.

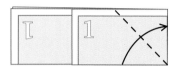

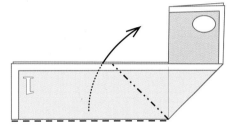

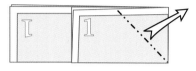

6. Squash-fold the top flap.

4. Valley-fold the bottom, folded edge of the front flap up to match the right edge of the paper.

5. Replace the layer to the bottom.

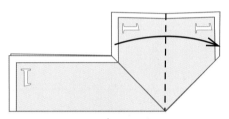

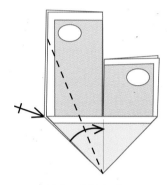

7. Valley-fold the left half of the squashed flap over to the right.

8. Squash-fold the left half of the model.

9. Valley-fold the bottom left folded edge the center crease. Repeat behind.

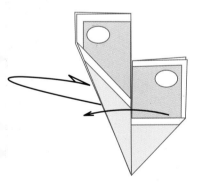

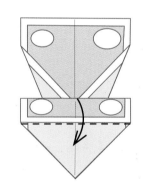

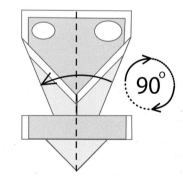

10. Rearrange the flaps so that both of the shorter ones are in the front and the longer ones are behind.

11. Valley-fold the top edge of the front flap down to the level indicated by the red line in the drawing.

12. Valley-fold the indicated flap down, forming the canard.

13. Valley-fold in half, lengthwise. Turn 90 degrees clockwise.

14. Valley-fold the wing sets down on each side of the fuselage. Set the wings out to the side to prepare for flight!

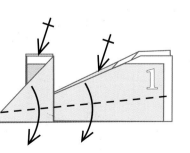

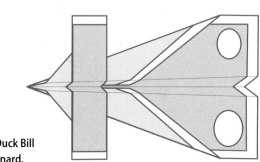

15. The Duck Bill Dollar Canard.

AIRPLANE #28
THE MAPLE SEED

By Michael G. LaFosse

By 1978 I had begun in earnest to design a series of origami planes for publication. I went through many reams of paper while refining my designs; all of which were folded from squares, trimmed from US letter paper. Now faced with piles of leftover strips, I wondered what I could fold with them. I found inspiration that spring during a walk in the Berkshires. The result is this Maple Seed.

Use paper from trimming 8 ½ by 11-inch sheets into squares. You can also try this model with other, similar rectangles.

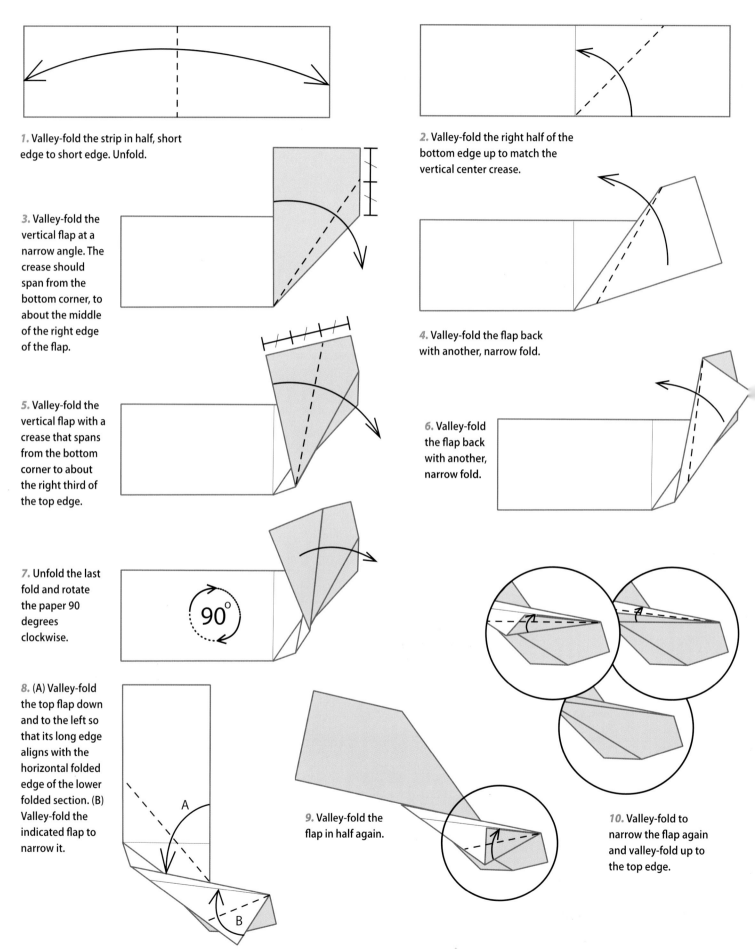

1. Valley-fold the strip in half, short edge to short edge. Unfold.

2. Valley-fold the right half of the bottom edge up to match the vertical center crease.

3. Valley-fold the vertical flap at a narrow angle. The crease should span from the bottom corner, to about the middle of the right edge of the flap.

4. Valley-fold the flap back with another, narrow fold.

5. Valley-fold the vertical flap with a crease that spans from the bottom corner to about the right third of the top edge.

6. Valley-fold the flap back with another, narrow fold.

7. Unfold the last fold and rotate the paper 90 degrees clockwise.

90°

8. (A) Valley-fold the top flap down and to the left so that its long edge aligns with the horizontal folded edge of the lower folded section. (B) Valley-fold the indicated flap to narrow it.

A

B

9. Valley-fold the flap in half again.

10. Valley-fold to narrow the flap again and valley-fold up to the top edge.

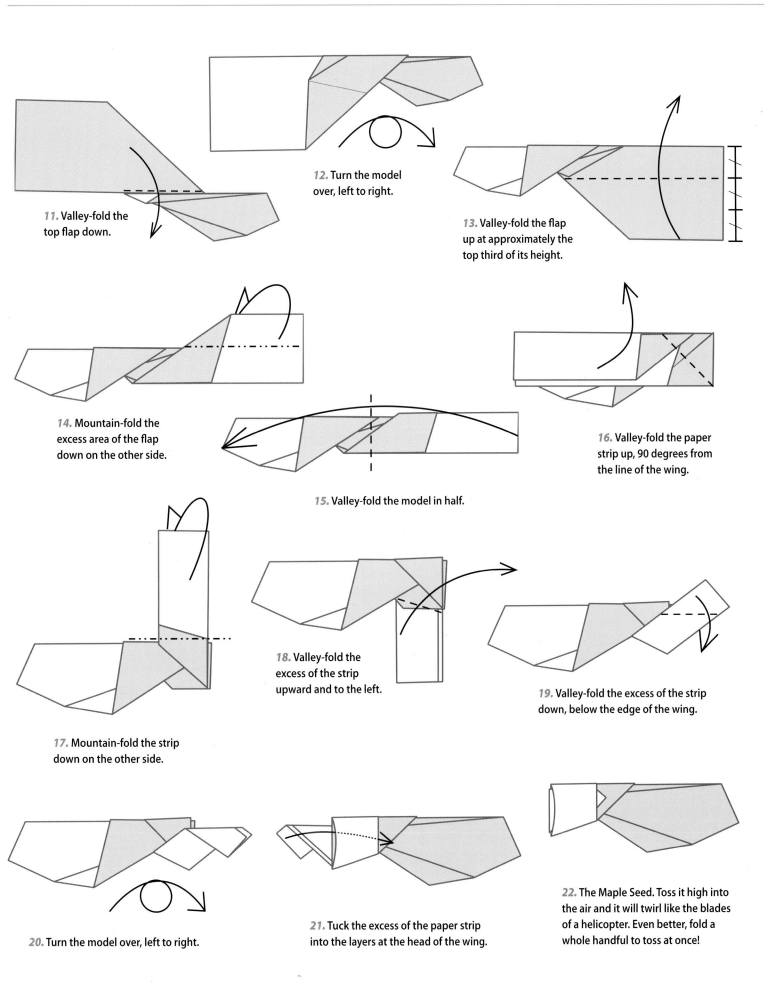

11. Valley-fold the top flap down.

12. Turn the model over, left to right.

13. Valley-fold the flap up at approximately the top third of its height.

14. Mountain-fold the excess area of the flap down on the other side.

15. Valley-fold the model in half.

16. Valley-fold the paper strip up, 90 degrees from the line of the wing.

17. Mountain-fold the strip down on the other side.

18. Valley-fold the excess of the strip upward and to the left.

19. Valley-fold the excess of the strip down, below the edge of the wing.

20. Turn the model over, left to right.

21. Tuck the excess of the paper strip into the layers at the head of the wing.

22. The Maple Seed. Toss it high into the air and it will twirl like the blades of a helicopter. Even better, fold a whole handful to toss at once!

CHAPTER 5
HOSTING A PAPER
AIRPLANE COMPETITION

Cheering crowds, the great outdoors, an exciting competition, and time spent making memories with good friends old and new—these are the hallmarks of a great paper airplane competition. Hosting a paper airplane competition can be an exciting and rewarding experience, or a stressful and unpleasant one. Planning saves time and money and organization helps minimize the frustration for all involved. If you ever want to host another competition, you had better plan and organize your first event well, because your first event becomes your public reputation. The following information will help you put together a fun and memorable event.

Organize and Energize a Team

Life is all about making lasting friendships and healthy relationships. Organizing a paper airplane contest is a great way to make some new friends and get your old friends involved. When you involve many talented people, everyone will enjoy the experience and share in the satisfaction of an event well done. The first step is to assemble a team. A planning team will include you, and at least two other people who share your enthusiasm. How many team members make the ideal team? It all depends upon their capabilities and how well you can coordinate their actions. Four or five people can handle a task like this quite easily. You may know many friends or family members who are willing to help. If you work at a large company, school or museum, you may have coworkers and staff members willing to help. Ask around about any local paper airplane experts that might be willing to help your team. Most airports, engineering colleges or technical design companies have paper airplane enthusiasts who are more than willing to share their favorite designs and experiences.

Above all, you need some people that know a lot of other people! Mix up the ages and backgrounds of people on your team. Remember that older people have already done things that you haven't done (they call it experience). Younger members may know more about how to use technology (such as social networking) to tap into huge networks of people who can help accomplish the team's mission. Imagine how much you will learn from a diverse group of enthusiasts; everyone will benefit greatly from the varied knowledge and perspectives.

Tap Into Community Resources

Perhaps your community already has an established system of organizing community events. There might be a school, library, museum, church, civic center, or recreation department. Often these professionals are looking for new ways to bring people together to enjoy the community resources and talents. Sometimes they coordinate fund-raising for worthy causes, and may even know of grants or sponsorships available for fun, educational, community gatherings. Your contest may become part of a larger celebration, drawing more attendees than they might have otherwise attracted.

Which Type of Contest Is Right for You?

For Open Design contests, consider grouping entrants into categories of styles: Darts, Wings, Rings, and Canards (those with forward wings). All of the entries must be single piece, no cuts, and no appliances.

It is simpler to limit the contest to a single type and size of airplane; *Single Design*. Most attendees will want to show off their own creations. Holding Single Design contests work great if you include a folding workshop before the event, and have plenty of paper stock for all entrants to fold a plane of uniform size, shape and weight. Make a category for whatever makes sense: Appearance, Distance, Folder Age or Level. You can also leave the size criteria open, and be surprised at what arrives. For the Single Design contest, we usually award prizes in three categories: Distance, Time Aloft, and Appearance. Single Design events can be part of a larger event. You can also announce the Single Design feature months in advance for contestants to hone their folding and flying skills for the selected design, using a paper of their choice.

Select the Venue

Think about the perfect place to enjoy paper airplane fun. It may not be in your grandmother's antiques parlor, but it may be on a big lawn in a park, the school gym, an empty parking lot, or even in a barn. My house has an upper deck looking out over 75 feet of lawn sloping down to a wide bend in the mighty Merrimack River. An airplane launched from this vantage point seems to hover forever while gentle breezes waft up the lawn from across the water. For your contest, consider spectator arrival and comfort. Is there a good viewing area? The great outdoors is free, but plan around the weather. Wind or rain can cause trouble. A large, enclosed space, such as a shopping mall is fine, and an innovative manager should welcome the added customers and community good will, while guiding you through specific ways to address their corporate safety policies and other concerns.

Identify Key Tasks

Edit, develop, and give a copy of the full task list to each team member. Divide tasks to evenly spread the responsibilities according to each team member's talents and abilities. Make it fun. Encourage each team member to think about their goal, and then list the necessary tasks that must be accomplished to reach their goal. List the resources and talent needed to accomplish each task.

Place initials next to the tasks that each feels comfortable learning and doing. Agree on a written deadline for each task with the team leader responsible for that task. Assign two dates to each task. The first is a progress report date for the task leader to identify any issues or needs so the group can have plenty of time to address options. The second is the drop dead due date by which key decisions and actions must be taken without jeopardizing the event.

Which tasks will require the most help? Who are some of the people you know who can help you properly handle those tasks?

Here's a sample task list:

- Appoint planning team members and hold meetings.
- Identify a charity or not-for-profit cause.
- Identify and work with sponsors.
- Select a suitable place and assign a venue liaison to check on the necessary services: electrical outlets for printer and computer, public address system, etc. Will you be holding a folding workshop? If so, you will need tables (and chairs) for folders to use.
- Plan how to handle traffic safety and car parking.
- Set a date, time, and rain date for the event.
- Establish the rules for the contest.
- Identify a Master of Ceremonies.
- Assign a Rules Committee to recruit participants and handle all registration categories, and entrant relations.
- Select the plane designs you want to teach and fly. Decide if there will be folding demonstrations, instructions, folding video workshops, etc.
- Recruit judges and judging guidelines (bring measuring tape, masking tape).
- Coordinate advertising and public relations tasks. Plan the advertising, create and place attractive notices and posters. Write and distribute press releases (Who, What, Why, When, and Where?).
- Obtain necessary donated materials: recycled paper, prizes and awards, etc.
- Organize the presentation of all prizes and awards. Can you set up a table to display the awards before and during the competition? People will need things to do

or to look at while they wait to compete.
- Line up safe refreshment donations, and a suitable area for them.
- Arrange adequate seating for contestants and spectators.
- Scout out restrooms and acquire supplies your guests will use (bathroom tissue, soap, hand towels).
- Consider providing a practice area for last minute fine tuning and trimming.
- Decide how to securely handle cash (register, or cashbox, change, receipts, etc.).

As you all divide and accept responsibilities, remember that the team leader has the big picture in mind, and sees to it that all of the essential, assigned jobs are being done properly and on time, by working among the various committees, while specifically not coming between the team and other parties in the public. Organizational skills are important, and if you don't have them, organizing this event will help you develop them. Learn to use the tools of teamwork.

Brainstorm past Planning Roadblocks

One of the most useful problem-solving techniques involves brainstorming with your team. This is a common technique used not only for problem solving, but also for product design and manufacturing. The rules of brainstorming are simple:

- Respect each member by allowing only one person to speak at a time. An easy way to do this is to use a *speaker's stick*. Only the person holding the speaker's stick may speak. (This might be actually be a pen, or another common object, that you can pass on to the next speaker when you are through speaking.) Somebody who wants to speak may hold out their hand for the speaker's stick, indicating to the current speaker that they would like to speak when the speaker has finished their point. If a speaker abuses possession of the speaker's stick, the team may hold a vote for a speaker's time limit of perhaps 2 minutes.
- A "scribe" (also called clerk, note taker,

secretary, or recorder) has the job of simply taking notes, accurately writing down who spoke, and what point or major idea each speaker made, without injecting any of their own evaluations or judgments.
- All of the team members should resist the impulse to evaluate any of the ideas before all are presented.

Research involves finding facts about each of the ideas that might improve the level of understanding to the point where clear choices can be made. Have the team members determine what data is important, and then guide them through finding the information.

Suggested Contest Rules

Your contest will need rules to create winners. Here is a suggested list of rules to help create a level playing field:

- Each entry must be only paper (plant fiber), folded and flown by the entrant. No other materials such as plastic, wood, or metals are allowed.
- Each entry must be folded from a single sheet of paper, with the following restrictions:
    Shape _____
    Size_____
    Weight _____
    Printing or graphics_____
- No cutting or tearing.
- No fasteners of any type, such as paste, tape, paper clips, glue, etc.
- No additional materials to add weight, such as dirt, pennies, or moisture.
- Only two throws allowed.
- Judges' ruling is final.

Lining Up Prizes and Awards

You can't have too many prizes and awards! Identify and coordinate with local stores, libraries, salons, restaurants, and shops that are willing to give you a small item or gift certificate in exchange for your mention of their business sponsorship at the event.

You will also use lots of paper. Incorporate recycling into your plans, and start collecting printer paper, magazines, and other free stock that can be recycled again after your contest is over. Decide if a particular type or size of paper will be required. If you have boxes of donated, recycled office paper, why not use it as is, rather than cut it square?

Offering Refreshments

Keep it simple. Don't run the risk of making anybody sick with perishable, homemade foods, but packaged crackers, cookies, or bottled water and soft drinks may be easy to offer to your contestants and spectators at the event. Charge at least a token amount to prevent some people from overindulging. Have more than one source of key items and supplies, just in case somebody forgets to bring something.

Communications, Press and Promotion

Make a sample event poster that you can show to the managers at your local bank, supermarket, library, or other place that most people visit. It should answer the basic questions of Who, What, Why, When and Where, while also communicating excitement. If the poster does not elicit an immediate, positive response, revise it to make it more appealing.

Write a short press release for your local newspaper(s). Give them plenty of time so they can decide when to cover your story. Many papers require a 2-week notice. Buy a paper and write down the names of the editor, likely reporters, and photographers you will be working with. Email them with an introduction and offer to meet with them at their convenience. Invite the reporter and photographer to the event.

Create a "flyer"—a paper airplane of your choice that can be decorated with contest information so that when it is printed and folded from brightly colored papers, the wings will do your advertising.

Make pre-event appearances to local clubs and organizations. Your community probably has various churches, a Chamber of Commerce, Rotary, Elks, Kiwanis, 4-H Clubs, Scouts, or other civic organizations

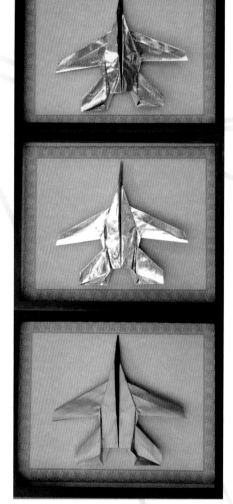

Framed origami airplanes, in colored foil to represent first, second and third place awards, are easy and inexpensive to customize and produce. These handmade keepsakes will be highly prized.

chartered to benefit the community standard of living. Specifically invite all their members. Provide an email invitation they can forward to their members, but respect their rights to not contact members by email directly. Consider selling advertising spaces in an attractive, souvenir program guide and rule book.

Get your updates onto social media. This is also a great way to ask for help, but be careful. If you're under 18 years old, have an adult watch how you use these powerful, but sometimes dangerous new tools.

Brush up on your technique. So you only know how to fold the classic dart? This book will introduce you to a host of folding and paper airplane design techniques that we have used and enjoyed for decades to produce some amazing performers. Master these projects and then mix and match some of the techniques to wow the crowds with your own concoctions.

Attendee, Volunteer and Sponsor Appreciation

Flying a paper airplane is much like listening to music, or watching a dance—an ephemeral joy, a fleeting moment. You can help make the enjoyment last by linking the fun to a tangible object, such as an event photo, trophy, or prize. The best way to ensure that attendees remember the fun they had—and not only share their experiences with friends, but return with those friends to your next event—is to reinforce the memory. Here are some ideas to extend the release of endorphins:

- Ask a responsible adult to videotape the contest and post the highlights on a shared website.
- Take plenty of action photographs for the local newspapers and media outlets, and be sure to pass out slips for people in the photos to neatly spell their names the way any attributions or captions should read.
- These slips should also grant publishing rights for your organization to use images of participant(s) in photos supplied to the news media.
- Obtain donated prizes from sponsors, such as gift certificates, Offer plenty of awards in several categories.
- Neatly fold and frame coveted paper airplane designs (such as the F-14 Tomcat) to be presented as top place trophies to the winners.
- Grant all participants, sponsors, and volunteers certificates of appreciation for their participation.

Opening and Closing Ceremony Scripts

Public speaking is difficult for many people. The following script can help you organize your thoughts and reduce stress when welcoming a group to your event.

Opening Ceremony Script

Welcome to the _____ Paper Airplane Contest!

My name is _____ and I will be your host.

(At this point, ask all the volunteers, sponsors, and team members to come up and take a bow. Introduce each by name.)

This event would not have been possible without the hard work of the following people: _____

Sponsors: _____

Thank you for: _____

Today we are pleased to welcome our special guests: _____

Please observe the rules of the contest: _____
_____
_____
_____

Refreshments are available: _____

The drinking fountain is: _____

The restrooms are located: _____

The prizes have been donated by: _____

A word about safety: Please be careful. This is no place for horseplay or running. The nose of an airplane may be only paper, but it is sharp, and could injure someone if you are not careful. Do not toss your airplane in any way that could injure anybody.

Please respect each other and each other's airplanes, and please have fun!

~

All good things must come to an end. Make sure you give your attendees a rousing send-off before they begin to disperse.

Closing Ceremony Script

Thank you all for coming!

Thanks again to all our sponsors: _____
_____

We would appreciate any of you who can stay a few moments to help us clean up this space and put it back the way we found it.

Our local paper airplane club meets _____ You are all welcome to attend.

Please tell your friends to watch for our next event!

It is easy to create forms for your judges to use to keep track of contestants' performances. Use large, easy-to-read type and keep the form simple to use.

Contestant Application for the

PAPER AIRPLANE COMPETITION
at the
PEABODY ESSEX MUSEUM
Salem, Massachusetts

May 22, 1994

CATEGORY OF COMPETITION	DATA
DISTANCE	
TIME ALOFT	

Best in Show consideration ☐

REGISTRATION

NAME: _____ AGE: _____
ADDRESS (optional): _____

FIRST PLACE
DISTANCE

Awarded to _____

for outstanding achievement in the Paper Airplane Competition

conducted at _____

on this day _____ *of* _____ *in the year of* _____.

_____
Senior Judge

Award forms should be printed on a heavyweight, high-quality paper. Once a certificate's design is created in a computer it can be saved and quickly customized for future events.

APPENDICES

A LONG-WINDED WORD ABOUT THE AIR

Let's take a moment to appreciate Earth's unique atmosphere that we simply call "the air." Go outside on a clear day and look up at the blue sky. Perhaps puffy white clouds are changing shapes in interesting ways. At sunrise and sunset, marvel at the brilliant hues of red, orange, and purple. If we were trying to do this on nearly any other spinning planet, there might not be anything to look at except stars punctuating a black shroud of nothing, or swirling clouds of poisonous gas.

Thanks to Earth's plants' propensity to fix carbon into chains of cellulose, their excess free oxygen and water vapor has left our atmosphere beautiful and visible, breathable, and laden with enough mass (substance) to allow birds, bats, bugs, butterflies, and even blimps to fly from place to place. It's air's mass that allows paper airplanes to do anything other than drop unremarkably.

Air is a mixture of many gasses, vapors, and particulates. Air is mostly nitrogen (about 80%), and oxygen (about 16%), which are both elements, but more importantly to the airplane enthusiast, air also contains various amounts of a gaseous compound, hydrogen dioxide (H_2O)—also more commonly known as water vapor. "Wet" air has more water vapor, as well as droplets of condensed water vapor (mist), and at high altitudes,

even microcrystalline frozen mist, all of which makes it heavier. Warm air can hold more moisture than cold air, but given the same moisture content, cold air is heavier than warm air, and flows down the river valleys from the mountains in cool breezes called *Chinooks*. Since the sun only heats half of our planet at a time as it twirls on its axis, when the sun reaches its highest point in the sky at noon, the molecules of air directly below it (and any water molecules) increase their level of motion (called heat). Some of the liquid water vaporizes, and the warmer air now contains more water vapor. As the sun sets, the same moist air mass cools and dries out at night, shedding its excess water vapor as condensed precipitation: mist, fog, snow, dew, or rain.

Paper is made from plant cellulose, an absorbent, highly porous substance greatly affected by moisture in the air. As such, it can quickly change its water content. Air is a fluid, as is liquid water, and fluids take the shape of their container, and can flow from place to place in response to imparted forces, such as gravity, when uncontained.

Unlike liquid water, air can be compressed. Every day, your TV weather reporter talks about high pressure or low pressure systems, or huge masses of hotter or colder air moving about the Earth. When different masses of air collide, the

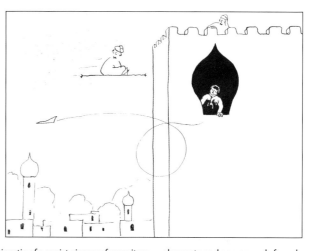

inertia of a moist air mass forces it up into collision with colder air masses. As the warm air cools, it sheds its condensed water vapor as snowflakes or raindrops. Different masses of air interact at their boundaries, called fronts, causing rain, wind, or generally bad weather. Similarly, heat absorbed by dark surfaces, such as roads, buildings, and paved parking lots, expands the air over those hot areas, causing convection currents of rising air, called "thermals." Toss your paper airplane out a window above a sun-soaked parking lot and watch how much farther it travels, compared to tossing it out of the window above a cool, shaded lawn.

Although both air and water are fluids, air is much less dense than liquid water because air molecules are much farther apart. Molecules of gas and vapor have more energy than molecules of the same

elements and compounds found as liquids or solids. That energy gives gas and vapor molecules "elbow room", or a relatively huge amount of space between the molecules. This allows us to compress air, making it denser. Think of the atmosphere as a container of air with a ball inside (the earth). Outside the container is nothing but empty space. Since air has mass, it is held close to the earth by simple gravity. This is our atmosphere, and sunlight bouncing off the air particles gives our atmosphere a blue luminescence when viewed from below. Fluids flow around obstructions, and air currents obstructed by buildings, fences and trees, produce swirling eddies in some spots, and strong, laminar flows in others. Try to sail your airplane between two buildings. Does it fly farther in one direction? Thank these qualities of fluids.

PAPER AIRPLANE TERMS AND JARGON

Aileron — A control surface, usually outboard on a wing's trailing edge, designed to increase drag on the wing for imparting a rolling motion, or applied in conjunction with rudder for a coordinated turn.

Airfoil — Shaped body (e.g., wing or prop blade) designed to create lift when in motion relative to surrounding air. The geometry of the cross section of an airfoil dictates its performance under various conditions of airflow and the angle of attack.

Angle of attack — The angle between the direction of airflow and the wing chord (straight line connecting the leading edge and trailing edge points on a wing cross section).

Anhedral — The angle between the lines along the two wings' upper surfaces when the wings' tips are lower than the wings' roots.

Appearance — Level of appeal to the judge, based solely upon visual factors.

Attitude — The position of an aircraft determined by the relationship of its axes and the horizon. e.g., the pitch attitude is the angle formed by the line straight through the fuselage (connecting nose and tail), and the line between tail and horizon indicating a level position.

Balance — Distribution of mass equally across a line of reference.

Balance Point — One point from which a paper airplane can be supported, so it stays in a level attitude compared to the horizon. (Also called the *center of gravity*, and often the desired point of release for a launch.)

Canard — The French word for "duck," used to describe a small, forward wing resembling the flat duck's bill, incorporated into designs favored for their stall resistance.

Density — The mass of a substance per unit of volume. e.g., grams (unit of mass) per cubic centimeter (unit of volume). For water, this is 1.0 gr/cm^3.

Dihedral — The angle between the two wings' upper surfaces when the wings' tips are higher than the wings' roots. A dihedral of 180 degrees would describe wings that are straight across, or parallel to the horizon. (A paper dart's dihedral angle changes when the plane is thrown and the fuselage opens.)

Distance — Linear measurement from contestant's toe to the nose of the airplane after it lands.

Drag — Force acting upon an airplane opposite to its direction of motion.

Elevator — A horizontal airfoil designed to control pitch (nose up or down), often located on the trailing edge of hind wing or airplane's tail, but also used on the trailing edge of a canard (forward wing).

Elevon — Combination elevator and aileron.

Endorphins — Natural chemicals that the brain released when you fold and fly paper airplanes that make you feel joy or pleasure.

Exposed surface area — Measurement in square inches of exposed paper on an airplane. When expressed as a percentage, the area of the paper that would be painted, compared to the total area of paper, if the folded model were to be painted, and then unfolded.

Flap — Movable extensions of the trailing edge of a wing, usually mounted close to the fuselage, designed to greatly extend the length of the airfoil, primarily used in takeoffs and landings.

Fuselage — The body of an aircraft, holding passengers, cargo and crew.

Laminar airflow — Streamlined flow of air in a zone of minimal turbulence near a boundary surface, such as a wing or canard.

Lift — Upward force generated by air flowing across a wing.

Mass — The quantity of matter that something contains that causes it to have weight in a gravitational field.

Pitch Adjustment — Change in position about the lateral axis. Raising or lowering the plane's nose while doing the opposite to the tail, causes a change in pitch attitude. To add pitch a pilot will push the stick back, nose up, flaps down (speed slows). To reduce pitch: stick forward, nose down, flaps up (speed increases).

Relative Humidity (RH) — The actual amount of water vapor contained in air, compared to the maximum amount of water vapor possible at that temperature. (When the RH reaches 100%, any additional moisture becomes fog, mist, rain, snow, or ice!)

Roll Adjustment — Change in position about the longitudinal axis. The continuous application of raising or lowering a wing, while doing the opposite to the other wing, causes a tight, corkscrew flight.

Spoiler — A control surface designed to diminish the lift on a wing. A spoiler raised on a high wing is one way to level the craft.

Stall — Sudden loss of lift caused by insufficient airflow over an airfoil, causing the airplane to drop.

Symmetry — Distribution of area compared across a line of reference.

Temperature — A measure of heat content.

Time aloft — Time in seconds between the airplane's leaving the contestant's hand and its contact with anything else (e.g., the floor).

Turbulence — Irregular motion of the paper airplane caused by erratic airflow.

Wing Root — The beginning of the wing at the fuselage (part of the wing farthest from the wing tip).

Yaw Adjustment — Change in position about the vertical axis. Turning the nose of the plane left or right, while doing the opposite to the tail of the plane, usually by changing the angle of the rudder or vertical stabilizer, turns the attitude of the plane left or right. Coordinated turns in a real, 3-axis controlled plane combines roll and yaw, for example, as the pilot rocks the stick to the right while applying right rudder (usually with a foot control), the plane banks and turns right while keeping the gravitational force on the pilot consistent. Yaw adjustments are also used to handle crosswinds upon landing, in a maneuver called "crabbing."

RESOURCES

British Origami Society
Membership Secretary
Penny Groom
2A The Chestnuts
Countesthorpe,
Leicester
LE8 5TL
UK
www.britishorigami.info

Centro Diffusione Origami
www.origami-cdo.it

Japan Origami Academic Society
c/o Gallery Origami House
1-33-8, Hakusan #216
Bunkyo-ku, Tokyo
113-0001, JAPAN
www.origami.gr.jp

OrigamiUSA
15 West 77 Street
New York, NY 10024-5192
www.origami-usa.org

Origami Organization Directories
www.origami-usa.org/groups_us
www.origami-usa.org/groups_international

Origamido Studio
www.origamido.com

WHAT'S ON THE DVD

The DVD included inside the back cover of this book provides detailed, step-by-step video lessons for each of the 28 amazing origami planes presented in the book. The graceful gliders, the sleek darts, and the exotic hybrids are all clearly demonstrated from the first fold to the last—you'll find that no fold is too complex when you're able to see, and fold along with master origami artist Michael G. LaFosse as he recreates each plane and provides expert advice. Pause and replay the steps to move through each lesson at your own pace.

ACKNOWLEDGMENTS

We thank our editor, Jon Steever, and his home-grown group of critics—his kids! We also thank Scott Duval at E-K Media, who made our DVD easy to use. We thank all who helped at paper airplane folding workshops and contests, especially Janey Winchell and Ellen Soares (at Peabody Essex Museum, Salem, MA), and OrigamiUSA volunteers such as Jonathan Baxter (Emcee and Supreme Judge at annual contests).

We are grateful to Darren Jacklin, Tom Wallman, Doris Weissacher, and Hangar-7 for permission to use a photo from Michael's origami airplane event at the Masters of Origami exhibit, (photo on page 5) held at Hangar-7, Austria, ca. 2005. We thank our dear friend Paul Rossi for the amusing and artful pen and ink drawings that grace several pages of this book (Paul drew these cartoons for Michael back in 1979, in anticipation of Michael's pending origami airplane book! At long last, they are joined!). Finally, we must thank the Alexander and LaFosse families, especially Gerard and Norman LaFosse (Michael's dad and uncle) who got Michael off to a good start!

PHOTO CREDITS

Darren Jacklin (www.jacklinfotos.com): page 5; Richard L. Alexander: All other photographs.

Pen and ink character drawings shown on pages 17, 18, 22, 23 and 94 are by Paul Rossi (www.paulrossiarts.com).

STACKED OVER LOGAN—PAGE 24

FLYING FOX—PAGE 44

F-102 DELTA JET—PAGE 47

TRANSFUSION—PAGE 56

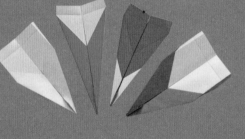

LOCK NOSE DARTS—PAGE 59

ART-DECO WING—PAGE 30

STORMIN' NORMAN—PAGE 41

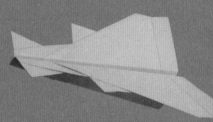

CANARD CRUISER—PAGE 74

LOCK NOSE DART: US LETTER A—PAGE 60

STDC—PAGE 81

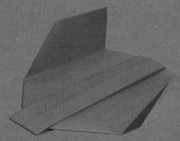

FINGER WINGER—PAGE 28

F-14 TOMCAT—PAGE 51

WHISKER JET—PAGE 83

ARROW—PAGE 35

DUCK BILL DOLLAR CANARD—PAGE 85